ANCHOR BOOKS

DISTANT SHADOWS

Edited by

Neil Day

First published in Great Britain in 2001 by
ANCHOR BOOKS
Remus House,
Coltsfoot Drive,
Peterborough, PE2 9JX
Telephone (01733) 898102

All Rights Reserved

Copyright Contributors 2001

HB ISBN 1 85930 980 1
SB ISBN 1 85930 985 2

FOREWORD

Anchor Books is a small press, established in 1992, with the aim of promoting readable poetry to as wide an audience as possible.

We hope to establish an outlet for writers of poetry who may have struggled to see their work in print.

The poems presented here have been selected from many entries. Editing proved to be a difficult task and as the Editor, the final selection was mine.

I trust this selection will delight and please the authors and all those who enjoy reading poetry.

Neil Day
Editor

CONTENTS

Feelings	J Smyth	1
The Fight	Tom Syron	2
Untitled	Suzy Talbot	3
The Call	Malcolm Wilson Bucknall	4
The Man In The Corner	Laura Conn	5
Ghost	T Searle	6
The Dolphin	Claire Nicole	7
When Did You Lose Your Father?	Denise Sackett	8
Edwin Gibbons God Speed	D P Deus	9
Voice Of The Tree	July Mortimer	10
Helen's Lament	Helen Millar	11
Pictures On The Wall	Janet Kelly	12
Untitled	Thelma Meadows	13
A Nice Cup Of Tea	S Brown	14
The Miracle House	Andrew Handsaker	15
Shipwrecked	Barbara Davies	16
My Love Sleeps	Roger Inglis	17
With A World-Wide Voice	Terry C Pallett	18
Morag	Elizabeth M Thom	19
I Love You	Jay Smith	20
To Be Home Again	Graeme Ross	21
Please Come Home	Kenneth Brown	22
Contentment	Linda Thurling	24
The Evensong Elves	Tracy Prime	25
Christmas Prayer	Dorothy Elizabeth Davies	26
A Mystery Unfurls	Elizabeth Wilkinson	27
Spirit Of Life	Sally Boyle	28
Living Each Moment	Bhavna Raithatha	29
The Millennium 2000	John Geehan	30
Life After Death	Beverley Munro	31
My Memory Of Matthew	David Thompson	32
Three Hundred Flies	M R Neve	34
Space Calling Earth	Mary Rhodes	35
The Gunfighter Fires A Blank	R Barbour	36
The Quest	M Mettam	37

Desire	Ross Stewart	38
Respite	R Probert	39
A Tune Forgotten	Patricia Hazel	40
Perrenporth Sands	Ian Brittle	41
The Leprechaun	Garry Knowles	42
Untitled	Kirstie Taylor-Moore	43
The Rival	Barbara Lovell	44
Shooting The Indians With Sticks	Kieth Jones	45
The Super Lady Of Mystery	Silva Stan	46
They	Chris Jones	47
New Year's Resolution	Arlene Skerratt	48
Deep Down	W W Foster	49
Water Or Love	Patricia Ferrari	50
Untitled	Daisy	51
Summer Morn	Phyllis Lorraine Stark	52
The Tramp	Linda Beavis	53
Homeless	Laura Cannon	54
In Polluted Cities Lined With Mould	M J Lloyd	55
Railway World	Noel Rainford	56
Stress	Agnes Cowan	57
Glackaphilip	Jim Doherty	58
Left Behind	Amy Wragg	59
Meadow Magic	Gillian M Ward	60
Survival Of The Luckiest	Tom Sawyer	61
Death's Executioner	C M Engler	62
The Evacuee	Rebecca Blackwell	63
Youth Remembered	Wilf Horner	64
A Private Journey	Neil G Hendry	65
The Sky	Shagufta Hussain	66
Synchronised Swimmer	Cathie Devitt	67
River!	Nicole Byrd	68
Why	Alison Gorton	69
The Universe	Lauren Heffer	70
Time	Richard Norburn	71
Mariana	Guy Moore	72

Thank You For Your Scraps - I'm A Very Grateful Chappie	Geraldine Varey	74
Pressure	N A Molyneux	76
Life	Roseanne Kelly	77
Today	Felicity Law	78
What I Believe	Mornee Gill	79
Felix Verus	Phillipa Adburgham	80
Blame It On The Weatherman	Peter Wilks	81
Photographs	Kathy Hill	82
The Sea	Alicia Baker	83
C'est La Vie	Michael Robertson	84
To Love	A G Trent	85
The Bunion	Gillian McNeish	86
What A Day	Ann Lacy	87
The One In Ten	Quintin Douglas	88
Death Of The Resuscitated	Michelle Wood	89
Easter Rising	Oliver Eadie	90
Just A Tree	Helen Barwood	91
You	Debbie Taylor	92
Life History	Mary Barville	93
Love	Kirsten Kearney	94
Breaking Through	C J Hatherall	95
The Seven Sisters	Lynda Morgan	96
Hope	Mona Brown	97
The Deer	Shaun Nash	98
Language Class	L Saunders	99
Feeding Rabbits	Wilson John Haire	100
I Wonder Why	Lynne Richardson	101
Plastic Vesicle	Laura Holt	102
The Country Lane	Vanessa Bell	104
Theodolite Terror	John Williams	105
My Primrose	V N King	106
A Melody Of Sound	Dorothy Irvine	107
Cat Love	Vera Jones	108
Alborada	Olive Yates	109
Miss You	Angie Wheeler	110
Forbidden Whisper	Richard Oliff	111
In Memoriam	David Wilson	112

The Precinct Is Neat	Peter Henry	113
Knowing Is Within	Jude Le Sage	114
A Little Word	Pam Spencer	116
If I Won The Lottery	Caroline Janney	117
Ticking Clock	Ruth Brigden	118
How Times Change	Rosemary Peach	119
Moving Day	Terry Rogers	120
School	Sophie Levi	121
The Birth	Mary O'Hara	122
Autumn	Sallyanne Hayes	123
The Lock Keeper	G R McCauley	124
Dark Of Night	Danny Coleman	126
A Happy Question	E M MacLennan	127
Sic Iter Ad Astra (Such Is The Way To The Stars)	Tom Crean	128
Untitled	Jaime-Louise Holmes	129
Untitled	Helen Setchfield	130
Northern Lights	Joy Thorpe	131
The Racing Pigeon	Brian Bates	132
Flecks Of Rain On My Face	Keith Lobban	133
Widow's Son	Seorsé De Sansaim	134
The Tale Of Mr Smithers	Cherrylyne	135
Father	Helen McAlinden	136
An Audience Of Cooks	N Donaldson	137
Do You Believe In God?	Derek Pile	138
Charlie	Joanna Carr	139
Exit To Heaven	R Burk	140
It's Time To Go	Margaret Monaghan	141
Caledonia	Julian Ronay	142
The Green And Pleasant Valley	P Loudon	143
My Life	D Woodford	144
Millennium	Ann Ogilvie	145
The Cottage Woodend	Johanna Nicoll	146
Old Lover's Lament	K D Lloyd	147
Accident	Sheila Matthews	148
What Work To Go To	Geoff Hunter	150
The Gift Of Life	Anibas	151
Missing Person - Person Found	Joy Jenkins	152

The Trenches - Lest We Forget	Margaret Lumsden	153
Does Springtime Still Come To The City?	Doris Payne	154
From Above The Sky	Anita Bowditch	155
Unable To Label Disabled	John Brook	156
What Am I	Pauline Dring	157

FEELINGS

When you're feeling really down
All screwed up inside
There's no escape, where you can run to
Nowhere for you to hide

When you're feeling all boxed in
Your life seems about to cave in
You cry for help, no one hears you
They must have all closed their ears

When you're feeling all alone
No one ever telephones
No one knocks upon your door
Or writes a letter to say they care

When the tears start to flow
You can't stop them, so let them go
Release the pain, the hurt inside
Then your pain will subside

When the pain runs much deeper
Tears won't come to your dry eyes
Though inside your soul is weeping
For loved ones eternally sleeping

Remember Him who soothes all pain
He gave His life so He could save you
He believes you're someone special
He will always be there for you

All you have to do is call Him
Let Him know that you want Him
He'll be there to give you comfort
Rely on Him, you can trust Him.

J Smyth

THE FIGHT

Horns are locked as they get set,
The two bulls fight, place your bet,
Their snouts are snorting, their blood boils,
Preparing to fight, to win the spoils.

Who will win, who will lose?
Where are the cheers, where are the boos,?
Who will lunge first, who will lunge last?
Will this fight be over fast?

Down goes one, what will he do?
Then he rises, welcomed by boos,
He then slams the other one into the floor,
The fight ends, the whole crowd roar.

Tom Syron

UNTITLED

I'm lying here in the middle of the night
Shivering, shaking and crying with fright.
I hear a shot; is it a friend?
When will all this fighting end?

NATO they have been and gone
They didn't stay for very long
It'll take years for all this hurt to mend
When will all this fighting end?

Thousands of people lying dead
Cruelly lined up and shot in the head
They were my family and my friends
I don't think this fighting will ever end.

All I hear is this stupid war
I don't want to hear it any more
Wherever I go it's always there
And to be honest I don't care.

Why are people so upset?
It's not us that it affects
I'm as content as I'll always be
Because, you see, it doesn't involve *me!*

What if you were dying out there
And no one really seemed to care?
Or if you were lying somewhere in pain
And people passed you again and again.

So you just ignore them dying and dead
Remove the thought from your head
But it could be you who's just been caught
So please, please spare them a single thought.

Suzy Talbot

THE CALL

Inside my heart, a restless tide is surging,
That draws me back again, down to the sea.
Unsettled still, I feel a sense and longing
To let again my anchor chains slip free.

Hypnotic sounds from passioned depths are calling,
Their crested beauty full of mystery.
Entice and beckon me with subtle gestures
To let again my anchor chains slip free.

I have no strength to still the rising passion,
That draws me back again, down to the sea.
The struggle in my heart, no longer fastened
As once again my anchor chains slip free.

Malcolm Wilson Bucknall

THE MAN IN THE CORNER

The man in the corner is never noticed
He's like the mist in the air
The insects on the ground
He sits there alone, crying
But no one stops to ask why.

The man in the corner has a story to tell
But only he knows it
The stories of his memories past
Of his little girl with hair so fair
And a loving wife who'd always been there
The memories of their death haunts him
He only wished he'd been there.

The man in the corner has no home, no life
People pass him on their way to their homes
While he sits there on his last breath
Now you know his story
But what does it matter
For the man in the corner
Was never there
He was like the breath on cold, fresh air.

Laura Conn

GHOST

Someone touched my hand
For one fleeting moment time stood still
Someone touched my hand
A half-forgotten promise
The solemn vow that lovers make
Someone touched my hand
This memory has come to me in person
My phantom love has sought me out
Someone touched my hand.

How cold time has made you
My spectre from my past
You transparent trick of light
Have you come to claim your ageless love
That we were cheated of
Someone touched my heart.

T Searle

THE DOLPHIN

As I wade out towards the deep, blue sea
A dolphin appears and swims straight for me
To experience the touch of its smooth, rubbery skin
Stirs in me, an energy within
The dolphin prods and pushes, gently with his nose
Encouraging us to go to the mysterious kingdom below
Water gushes everywhere, I feel like I'm drowning
My ears start drumming
My heart cannot stop thumping
Finding it hard to breathe, yet feeling so high
What's this magical feeling keeping me alive
Because what lies ahead, comes as such a surprise
To see an underwater city in full sunrise
Shown like a queen, being led through a dream
With dolphins, sea horses, mermaids and fishes
So many fantasies which will come true at my wishes
Huge, silver gates entwined in tropical flowers
These magnificent creatures with mystical powers
Out step the water babies from behind the rocks
Their pretty, round faces and curled, golden locks
Now not so shy, I see curiosity in their eyes
Smiling with sweetness as they whisper their secrets
Up swims a mermaid and takes my hand
We begin dancing to music, in this enchanting land
One of the babes runs up and hugs me so tight
My dolphin friend is waiting patiently in the light
The mermaid glides away, watching the flick of her tail
Knowing I have to leave behind this sweet fairy tale.

Claire Nicole

WHEN DID YOU LOSE YOUR FATHER?

'When did you lose your father?' they say,
'At fifty-two - tragic,'
I cough and make the noises they expect to hear,
But inside I am screaming, when did I lose him?

Was it the moment they stopped giving him cigars
and congratulations outside the delivery room?
Was it the first time he screamed and was cruel to me?
Was it the first realisation that he had feet of clay?

'When did you lose your father?'
Could I tell you the exact moment?
I don't think I could,
But it happened long before we laid him in the earth.

Denise Sackett

EDWIN GIBBONS GOD SPEED

Yes, God speed you,
Wherever you are going,
If it's to the lake isle
Of Innisfree.
Or if you are to become
A new star
In the morning sky,
God speed you.
With your special light
And your universal smile.
You were always immortal
And true.
I'll never believe that you've
Gone.
God speed you!

D P Deus

VOICE OF THE TREE

I am a big, strong tree,
But someone is shouting at me,
They're disturbing the peace of the wood,
I'd shut them up if only I could.

Timber the voice cries out,
The tree is falling; there is no doubt,
My neighbour, who was standing high,
Can no longer reach the sky.

The men with their machines are here,
They cut the trees down, this I fear,
My turn will be next, I'm sure I know,
But I do not want to go.

I was happy as could be,
Growing out there wild and free,
But now I'm felled I have to go,
To the factory this is so.

I'll be sawn and sanded too,
'Cause my trunk is useful to you,
I'm first class wood, there's no mistake.
Good furniture I will make.

Julie Mortimer

HELEN'S LAMENT

For weeks I've searched the shops
A present for you till I'm fit to drop.
I wanted something nice for your special day
Don't ask me what it was, as I can't say.
A list I wrote to try to help
A box of chocs, no they would melt
A cardigan, I could knit.
But couldn't find the time to sit.
A dress oh! that would be nice
But when I saw one, oh! what a price.
Maybe a hair-do, you could get
But there again, you might forget.
Good Lord what will I do?
The days that are left are so few.
It won't be long till your special day
What can I give? What can I say?
A happy birthday Aunty Teenie.
I'll just have to buy you a brand new peenie (apron)
For I am exhausted and have no more time
To find that special present of mine.
Wait, another idea, now I must decide
Please accept this watch and wear it with pride.
Now that I have made a decision
I'll continue on my special mission
To wash my face and get dolled up
Tonight's the night for a knees-up.

Helen Millar

PICTURES ON THE WALL
(In dedication of my Children)

As I look upon my photographs, that are laid across my wall
I'm surrounded with children, mine, the best of all.
Every picture tells a story of a very happy event
Of things we'd done together, where we've been and went.
There are many smily faces and some I guess are sad,
They're positive reminders of pets and friends we've had,
I sometimes look back over, as I smile, as I recall,
All those sweet memories of when each child was born.
What we've been through together, it's all been so worthwhile,
And now, they're both grown up, they still make me smile.
Over the 26 years, they've grown up good, strong and tall,
They're both married with children, my new babe's so small,
Yes, I am a Grandma, yes happy and so proud,
A Grandma 8 times over I want to shout out loud,
Even though I am so happy my tears they often sting,
As I wish my children could be little still
I miss them as my children, but now they are my friends
We still do things together, our friendship will never end,
I cannot kiss them better and the tooth fairy's gone away
But my dear Janine and Sonya, I love you more each day.
God bless.

Janet Kelly

UNTITLED

I wish that I could write a love song
That would tell him exactly how I feel,
I can't find the words to say
So I kneel down and pray
That some day he'll know how much I love him so,
That day will come and by his grace,
With outstretched arms I'll know the warmth of his embrace.
No need for words, for he will know,
The look upon my upturned face will tell him so.
Happy the bride upon that day
The bells will ring,
The people sing,
The children play,
Music fills the air, there's blossoms everywhere.
And joy and happiness for everyone to share.

Thelma Meadows

A Nice Cup Of Tea

Oh! I do like a nice cup of tea
I do like a nice cup of tea
While on frosty mornings before day is dawning
I do like a nice cup of tea.

My mum has a lie in on Sunday's
And leaves everything up to me
I shout up and ask her 'What would you like?'
She says, 'I would like a nice cup of tea.'

Dad comes home from work
He says his hello's to me,
Mum gets out the cups and saucers
And we then have a nice cup of tea.

I like mine just nice for drinking
Not too hot or too strong for me,
With three lumps of sugar, no tea leaves on top
Oh, I just like a nice cup of tea.

I often go visiting my Nana
She welcomes me always with glee
'Have a cup of coffee child'
'Thanks Nan, I prefer a nice cup of tea.'

Tea leaves from India and China,
Adverts galore plain to see,
My favourite brand has no matter
I just like a nice cup of tea.

S Brown

THE MIRACLE HOUSE

I fell prey to the miracle house,
Not expecting inanimate charms.
Enveloped like a sinner,
In a fallen angel's arms.

I glooped dazed into the miracle house
Through the porridge of confusion.
Gazed wide-mouthed at the poor decor
Of this unholy institution.

I slept fitfully in the miracle house,
Maniacally whirled in feverish dance.
Kept the miracle well hidden
Under the shirt tucked in my pants.

I was evicted from the miracle house
With prescriptions and with pain.
I tried to sneak another peek
But never set eyes on her again.

I pondered joys and woes of miracle house
That nagged gnat-like at my brain.
I came out with a miracle
But never saw her again.

Andrew Handsaker

SHIPWRECKED

A millpond sea in the quiet of night
Bathed in the glow of the moon's mellow light
Gentle sway of the ocean reaching forth to the land
Soft lapping of waves as they break on the sand.

Silvery glow spreading fingers of light
Where a ghostly shape rests in the silence of night
To reflect in the shadow of the old smuggler's cave
A skeleton ship in its watery grave.

In the old harbour tavern, he remembers so well
An old salt of the sea has a story to tell
His rheumy eyes misty as he sips at his ale
And for all who will listen he recalls a sad tale.

He tells of his comrades, men of his kind
For never again will he know peace of mind
His soul ever haunted, man of torment is he
Since the terrible night of the storm at sea.

Flashes of lightning, thunderclaps loud
Waves tall as houses, inky black cloud
A wild roaming spirit wanton and free
Tossing their ship as a cork on the sea.

Hurricane winds hit ocean and sand
Driving their vessel to a rock near the land
As a flimsy toy in the storm's mighty roar
Men's futile cries as they swim to the shore.

There was one who survived his own story to tell
He oft, in his wanderings hears the toll of ship's bell
Siren wails call him from over the sea
A man not at peace, restless spirit is he.

Barbara Davies

My Love Sleeps

I lost your sweet presence
In the glow of summer's embers
Through fading summer leaves
Dapple sunlight, sprinkled the ground.

When it was too late to appreciate
Time was so precious
The voice of the seasons
Now whisper your every thought.

Your lingering memory
Brings sunshine to each day that dawns
As you sleep with my love as your pillow
Embalmed by tears, in the warmth of my heart.

Roger Inglis

WITH A WORLD-WIDE VOICE

I have so much to say, but cannot find the right word,
To express my distaste, at all the killing, it's so absurd.
Unless it's money or something that's rewarding for its worth,
Man will slaughter and kill off the species and ruin our earth.

As animal lovers, we can only sit back and watch in grieving dismay,
Whilst our creatures and endangered species, are destroyed, day by day.
Hunting and killing, expressed as 'our heritage' and enjoyed by royalty,
But, what of the animals, how do they think, that's our first loyalty.

You'll hear them say, 'Hunt and shoot them, they're only a pest,'
Rewarded with blood-money, from whoever offers the best.
Right round the world, creatures with beautiful skin or fur
                                                     or magnificent horn,
Are butchered and slaughtered for profit, sometimes, quite soon
                                                     after they're born.

So I'd like to say these words, with a world-wide voice,
'We were all born to this earth, to who and where, we had no choice.'
I make my plea to you all, before it's too late,
'Think twice before you kill, leave them be, for everyone to appreciate.'

Terry C Pallett

MORAG

Hello, all! My name is Morag, my collar and lead are here
I'm going somewhere called the vet
My owner says there's nothing to fear.

We get in the car, I sit on my rug, I love to travel this way
I can curl up and sleep, or bark at the kids,
I wonder what I'll do today?

The journey is short, I slept all the time, about fifteen minutes, no more,
Up a long drive so full of smells,
I wonder what next is in store?

The doorbell rings, oh what a nice girl, our name, address, she takes
Then into a room, dogs, cats, rabbits and mice,
In a high cage, a yellow bird, a terrible noise it makes.

I sit on my owner's knee, I'm not allowed on the floor
I smile at a collie, perhaps a cousin,
She growls, now what was that for?

A cat peeps out of its wicker basket, ears back, is it scared like me?
A scruffy dog in the corner sits
It's scratching, perhaps a flea!

'You're a lovely puppy,' my next door lady smiles
She scratches my ear, I shake my head,
Then I lick her hand, what guile!

'Mrs Brown, Morag, your turn now,' I'm carried thro' another door
I sit on a table, then suddenly a sharp prick,
So that's what the vet is for!

Elizabeth M Thom

I Love You

I love you, each and every day,
I love you, as each night I pray,
I love you, as the day turns night,
I love you, in each morning's light,
I love you, just the way you are,
I love you, be you near or far,
I love you, more each single kiss,
I love you, for all time is bliss,
I love you, 'cause you are, just you,
I love you, a feeling oh so true,
I love you, for so many things,
I love you, how my heart it sings,
I love you, I whisper as you sleep,
I love you, a secret, I can never keep!

Jay Smith

TO BE HOME AGAIN

I stumble to my feet, the order given,
Shocked awake, I wipe my eyes of sleep.
I see the leader, face hard and driven,
Not quite twenty, age now begins to creep.
We are on the march yet again,
Forever fearful, the snipers' bullets await
Those less aware, eyes wet with rain.
Would I run if I knew my fate?
Where would I run? Danger everywhere
From men I know not, hate not,
But men I must kill, if I dare,
For if I fail, death is my lot.
This may be my last letter to you.
I'm ready for battle, I'm ready to die,
I've seen much death in the morning dew,
I've heard my friends choke on their death cry.
I believe the deaths of soldiers in battle
Give rise to their spirits, spirits which
Move unseen around us, their deaths not futile.
Oh! To be home again, young and rich
And if peace one day they should declare,
Make it a lasting peace we can share.

Graeme Ross

PLEASE COME HOME
(Jerome, aged 15, ran away from his home in Wales on January 1st 2001)

You ran away on New Year's Day,
And haven't been seen since then.
And my heart is grey, more than words can say,
And my life is a curse among men.
So come back my son, please come home . . .

Your mother and I have suffered our part
But never such torment and pain!
And never such worry and anguish of heart,
As to when we shall see you again.
So come back, my son, please come home . . .

Your sisters are stricken, your aunt is distraught,
And your grandma is out of her mind,
The police have no news and no clues to report,
And the neighbours still try to be kind.
So come back, my son, please come home . . .

You guardian angels, please give me the truth,
As to why you allowed him to go.
And you, God in Heaven, just give me some proof
That you care, that you care, for I do love him so:
Oh come back, my son, please come home . . .

I've been on my knees and I've prayed and I've prayed,
But got no reply from above.
And all I can plead are mistakes that I've made,
And tell him the depth of my love.
For I love you, my son: please come home.

And so through the night hours I send up my prayers
For the click of the latch or the ring of a phone,
Or the creak of the boards as you tiptoe upstairs,
For I love you so dearly, my son, my Jerome.
Yes, I love you so dearly - so please . . . come home!

Kenneth Brown

CONTENTMENT

Bathe, dress, perfume, tingle,
Excitement rising and ready to mingle.
Enter the club, goodbye to the fear,
Relaxing and laughing and having a beer.
Keep on smiling and trying to be friendly,
Why does everyone look so young and trendy?
Every track seems so loud and long,
They all sound the same, a never-ending song.
Here one comes, a potential man,
Talks of himself, his own greatest fan.
Suddenly no fun, just very dreary,
I've had enough, I'm tired and weary.
Trying to flutter my lashes and flirt,
All I can think is how my feet hurt.
12 o'clock strikes, Cinderella at the ball,
Realisation hits, I'm not enjoying this at all.
I'm going home, there's nothing to miss,
Time to exit gracefully and avoid a drunken kiss.
My friends agree, they like my choice,
Didn't want to leave first, I'm a unanimous voice.
Start the long walk home, but let's not be so hasty,
The best I've seen all night, now that I can call tasty.
A sigh of relief, satisfaction in sight,
Burger and chips, a great end to the night.
I lie down in bed, my ears are still ringing,
But somewhere inside I hear my heart singing.
I'm happy being me, I've nothing to prove,
A video and takeaway is what I'd rather choose,
Through tomorrow's hangover it will be clear to see,
Young and trendy clubbers can't wait to be like me!

Linda Thurling

THE EVENSONG ELVES

The man in the moon tonight is singing,
His face upturned in heavenly song,
The stars around are gently sending
The melodious notes of his song along.
Along, Along, and down to the glen,
Where the firefly fairies are merry and bright
Singing and dancing in gay abandon,
For the Evensong Elves have a party tonight!
Music and laughter will fill the air
While fairies chase the evening shadows,
Their friends in the forest will happily stir,
And gather to sing in the moonlit meadows.
They'll feast on acorns, honey and briar.
Whilst drinking their fill from the silvery stream.
Roasting nuts on the glowing embers,
What a moonlit, magical, mystical scene
Sweet the sound of them softly calling,
As they raise their voices to the dawning sun.
The morning is her curtains a-drawing,
Around them as they sing along.
The firefly fairies lead their friends homewards,
Gently glowing in the dawn's early light,
The elves curl up, under leaves - so tired,
And dream of the magic they made last night.

Tracy Prime

CHRISTMAS PRAYER

Christmas is the time of year when wars should be forgot,
When fighting stops and bombs cease to drop.
When people hold their hands out to all mankind,
In hope that their future should mean 'auld lang syne'.

Love should be abundant,
All around us everywhere.
Love to show our friends and family,
Just how much we care.

A greeting card a friendly smile is not a lot to ask,
Let's show all of mankind the love we should not mask.

For many this is a hurtful time
When cruelty has played its game,
When loved ones have left forever never to be seen again.

Hold out your hands and give a heart,
Don't turn and walk away,
Show mankind the love we share on this Christmas Day.

Oh Lord on high please hear our plea,
To make peace once more prevail.
Give us your love so we can expand and give a hand
each and every day.

Dorothy Elizabeth Davies

A Mystery Unfurls

The wonder of the night stars shine like jewels in the sky,
The moon glides across the sky in her silken gown,
Her face shines so bright for all to see,
Like a large searchlight so round and high in the clouds.
Suddenly a cloud appears across the lower half of the moon,
So peeping out is only half of her delight.
Slowly the earth moves a little more till the moon is out of sight.
As soon as the night went dark a glimmer of light appeared.
The earth she moves so the moon can roam
In beautiful heavens and shine her light far down below.
You'll have guessed it was a total eclipse of the moon.
As she begins to shine, first it's yellow then orange for all to see.
Some people say she was red before she sailed so free to
                                        continue her journey far away
And all the stars glistened and shone as if nothing had been
And this mystery of the world remained to delight us with her beauty.

Elizabeth Wilkinson

Spirit Of Life

How wonderful the life
Of all that is around,
How magical and wondrous,
The sight, each touch, each sound.
How powerful and vibrant,
The love that's deep inside,
How lucky in our times of need
We have our special guide.

May goodness and mercy stay with us
Through our earthly existence on land,
May we feel love's spiritual comfort
And God's love from the healing hand.
Help us understand, there is a forever,
Life's just adorning a different disguise,
That our spirit can perish never,
For the spirit never dies.

Sally Boyle

LIVING EACH MOMENT

Another hour passes
And the day
Turns into night.
Another day is over
It's time to rest and sleep.

What has happened
Has happened,
And we cannot
Change the past
Live each moment, as your last.

This little life
Doesn't offer much
We wonder through
Each stage of life
Not knowing what tomorrow brings.

What has happened
Has happened,
And we cannot
Change the past
Live each moment, as your last.

Life is a mystery
Dark and dangerous
Each day arrives, unexpected, unknown.
We take each day for granted
But, should we?

What has happened
Has happened,
And we cannot
Change the past
Live each moment, as it won't last that long . . .

Bhavna Raithatha

THE MILLENNIUM 2000

I stood alone beside a sea
A blue velvet of tranquillity
There upon that sandy shore
Which Father Time had made
Millions of souls had passed before
And decayed by decades.

Oh sentinel immortal
Magnificent mountain high
You reach to touch the sunset
That beautifies the sky

Then those rugged rocks
Which lurk among the mist
That shroud the craggy moor
Like tombstones for dead and gone
May last a million years or more
After humanity has passed on.

John Geehan

LIFE AFTER DEATH

Lies between two grey breeze blocks,
deep in the foundations
of my new extension.
A sealed cellophane pack
entombed between house and garage.
A packfull of my existence
in the millennium year.

Receipts of ploughman's lunches
from village pubs on sunny days.
- I always drove home
- he'd always want that extra pint
of dark Sussex ale.

And photos - my hair still long and red,
- his faded Levi's
And the children - he nearly seventeen
- khaki combats and black, black T-shirts.
She - fourteen - a leggy Lolita
flirting with the lens
in my green, green garden.
Ever fertile - tranquil refuge
echoes earlier sounds
of water fights - squirts and squeals.

When my bones are ash
these Polaroid images
that freeze my life in time
will endure.
I will live on
and I wonder . . .
if someone . . .
will wonder . . .
about me.

Beverley Munro

My Memory Of Matthew

There's wan memory of Matthew
Of that I wid like tae talk.
He wis jist a lad at the time,
When wie Chris and I, he did walk.
We took alang oor 'bogie'
Which we hid chance tae ride.
We wid pull it up tae the tap o' a hill,
And ride it doon the other side.
We came upon a hill sae big,
It gave us quite a scare.
We thought we wur tap o' Ben Nevis,
As we lukked doon frae there.
Chris wis the driver, steering wie his feet;
Matthew in the middle, hauding oan.
I wis the pusher at the back,
Sat on my hunkers; wance we got going
The 'bogie' sterted tae pick up speed,
And shin wis hurtling fast.
It felt like a hunner miles an hour,
As awe things flashed oan past.
A hazard came upon us quick,
Fur we wur approaching a corner.
Thank God thur wisnae a tractor coming,
We wid surely awe be a goner.
Alas this tale came tae a feenish,
And it his a sorry end.
Fur we did go doon anither brae,
That hid a gravel bend.
That's when Chris loast the steering,
We spun on oor side and crashed
And soon we awe sterted greeting.
Fur the wheels wur awe bent and bashed

So noo oor 'bogie's' gone tae rest;
Doon by a lochside tree;
Leaving the memory of Matthew,
Ferever in ma hert tae be.

Rest in peace, Matthew.
Your Uncle David.

David Thompson

THREE HUNDRED FLIES

Leggerty Peggerty a hairy old spider,
Wove a web that got deeper and wider.
He spun so hard with his silk sticky thread,
That three hundred flies all ended up dead.
Three hundred flies for his supper time treat,
That's far too many for a spider to eat.
It's a shame and a pity his tummy's so small,
Leggerty Peggerty can't manage them all.
So
Some he will save to enjoy Christmas Day,
Three hundred flies and not one got away!

M R Neve

SPACE CALLING EARTH

As an alien visiting Earth,
I speak without bias or mirth.
I have seen nothing worse, in the whole Universe,
Than the way you behave,
Destroy, rant and rave,
It seems like you're under some curse!

With so much to love and enjoy,
Certain well-meaning groups, do employ,
New ways to redress, this whole horrible mess
But the harder they try
It's the same raucous cry -
More money, more power, nothing less.

Very soon, with all animals dead,
Haggard human forms, looming, unfed,
Your whole rotten race, is in total disgrace,
You missed every chance
Your grim lives to enhance,
Before long, you'll be gone, without trace!

As for me - there's a warning
Distressing, yet clear.
Zoom back into space now -
And just - disappear!

Mary Rhodes

THE GUNFIGHTER FIRES A BLANK

Ensconced in a tavern
The overworked gunfighter
Did his evil thing
Then the girl walked in.

Hesitation would be fatal
But first another double scotch
He would have to test his metal
But of course steady on the rocks

The lone beauty stood at the bar
First another pint of ale
To his eyes she looked so far
Was he destined to fail

Another drink
He starts to swagger
Is he in the pink
No he only staggers

'Buy you a drink?' he mutters
She gives no answer
He starts to stutter
He is no dancer

A look of disgust
As she walks out the door
The gunfighter bites the dust
He would see her no more

No love or lust
Oh no the last bell
The gunfighter gone bust
Oh well, what the Hell!

R Barbour

THE QUEST

Come, find me, Friend,
Come, claim me now,
Before the long grey day is done,
Before cold winter comes.

I wear my solitude like a shield,
Come, seek me out, disarm me now,
Yes now, for even now is late,
The ebb tide fast recedes.

So come, Bold Conqueror of the night,
And take these brittle hands in yours,
Breath soft upon these stony lips,
Gaze rapt into these sculptured eyes,
And win this so indifferent heart.

M Mettam

DESIRE

Stumbling aboard all hassled and troubled,
Taking note of the people,
Knocked as I pass.
A young lady
Blonde, blue-eyed, beautiful!
Glancing invitingly
She records my presence.

All quiet now, calmed but excited
Belongings stored, sat down, opposite
Severely distracted, I read,
Missing huge chunks of news and text
I fumble with my paper,
She fumbles with her magazine.

Sitting up, I rock my leg, glance up,
She looks back, sits up still further
Our eyes meet
Wanting.

It happens repeatedly, once more, and again.

The loudspeaker calls out, 'Next stop Forres.'
Hell no, stay, please, please
Taking time to leave, making her point
Paper folded, no reason to read now,
Now she's gone.

Glancing in for the last time
Wrought with anger, pain on each other's faces,
Gone, she'll not be forgotten.

Life's too damn short,
Too short to be shy,
It's her damn loss,
As well as mine
Desire.

Ross Stewart

RESPITE

The sun is bright upon the lawn,
the grass with early dew is wet.
The nestlings twitter to the morn,
and, for a moment, I forget.

I breathe the scent of crimson rose,
the fragrance of the pale sweet peas;
My heart with tender worship glows,
and, for a moment, is at ease.

The pearly radiance of the sky,
foretells the beauty of the day.
A warm breeze frolics, whispering by,
and, for a moment, I am gay.

Begrudge me not this brief reprieve
from aching memory's bitter tears;
Too soon will clouds o'ercast the eve,
and anguish stalk the lonely years.

But now the day is dawning fair,
the healing scent of mignonette
steals like a balm upon the air,
and, for a moment, I forget.

R Probert

A Tune Forgotten

The tune may be dead but the melody lives,
The many years lead but not many reeves.
The crowd led cheerily on the day;
'Olé! Olé!'
Chanted on the way.

Off to celebrate;
Each with a mate,
To eat haggis and 'neeps'
As each wiggle the hips.
The tune had died;
Each to each confide.

The tune may be dead,
Yet the lyric's led,
'Oh Scotland! Oh Scotland!'
The land who gave . . .
All those men so brave.

Some at homes stately;
Some at homes simply,
Tables laid neatly;
As glasses raise to the head,
'Cheers to Robbie instead.'

Patricia Hazel

PERRENPORTH SANDS

When I was young,
I played upon the beach of life,
Building castles in the sand,
Or damming streams for fun,
But the tides of time wait for no man,
Overflowing our puny efforts.

When some were older,
They rode the white horses,
Thundering towards the land,
But I, like many stayed upon the shore,
Afraid of hooves and flying mane.

Now I am old,
And I walk upon the beach of life,
Watching the children play
And then comes second childhood, I'll play once more,
Get me a JCB!

Ian Brittle

THE LEPRECHAUN
(For Tim Smurf)

In County Cork I rode one day, on motorcycle I.
A summer's day it was quite warm, the sun high in the sky.
On gravel tyres began to slide, I looked for place to fall.
I landed hard upon the grass that's when I heard the call.
'Oh help me please I am in pain, my leg I think is broke.'
I looked around I could not see from where the voice had spoke.
'I'll try to help but where are you?' I stood and I did bellow.
'I'm here you fool, can you not see?' said the grumpy little fellow.
With beard of red and clothes so green, he was but two feet tall.
I walked towards the spot he lay, to where he'd had his fall.
'Well help me up you stupid man,' he snapped as I drew near.
'Here grab my hand you tedious fool, of me you need not fear.
Set me down upon that rock and then you must be gone.
Before you go a wish I'll grant, but mind you only one.
Be careful what you wish for Fool, for once it's done, it's done.
To spend your wish on foolish things, believe me won't be fun.'
I sat and thought of what I want, and then it came to me.
To ride my bike at breakneck speeds, that would give me glee.
'You are the fool I took you for; your pockets I know are empty.
Wealth and riches, women and booze, you can have with plenty.'
I was stern, to ride my bike, the others I need none.
He shook his head and waved his arm, a flash and he was gone.
I rode my bike towards my home at speeds not tried before.
On corners I did not slow down, but laid it on the floor.
I raced down hills along the straight, but as I passed a farm,
A flash came there before my eyes and someone touched my arm.
The Leprechaun sat upon my tank he couldn't work it out.
'Why this wish and not the others?' his little voice did shout.
I smiled at him and wound the throttle, the bike it did go faster.
I couldn't use the others my friend, for I'm the local pastor.

Garry Knowles

UNTITLED

Viewing the sky in all its
new world order.
Cocaine clouds kicking back
to enjoy the day.
With no heavyweight rain to
curse the acidic vapour
it will only be the sun that burns our
skin today.

Kirstie Taylor-Moore

THE RIVAL

Grandma has a new pet now - she gives it loads of fuss
It needs lots of her time, she says, but there's plenty left for us.
Santa Claus brought 'Snowy' as a Christmas Day surprise
Complete with cage - a snow-white budgerigar, with bright red eyes.
He's taken over Grandma's life, she's bought him bells to ring -
A ladder and some cuttlefish, a mirror and a swing.
He calls himself a 'Pretty Boy' and gives himself a kiss,
You'd never think a budgerigar could be as vain as this!
Every night it's 'flying time' - he zooms into the air,
Swooping round and round the lounge and landing in your hair.
He'll drink your cocoa, eat your crisps, he even steals your fruit.
He pecks your ear, and pulls your hair, but Grandma thinks he's cute!
He screeches when you're on the phone, he shouts and chirrups so
Competing with the telly, drowning out the Radio.
But when he's tired and sleepy, he's such a cuddly little thing.
I love the way he goes to sleep - his head tucked in his wing.
He stands on one leg on his perch, you'd think he'd slip and fall,
Then puffs his feathers out and looks just like a fluffy ball.
I know my grandma loves me, but I really can't be sure
Now Snowy's come to live with her, she loves the budgie more!

Barbara Lovell

SHOOTING THE INDIANS WITH STICKS

I never cried when my father died
Though it cut deep in my heart
Of all those memories that I have
Shooting the Indians with sticks
Is the one that I really treasure

No words of sympathy I would speak
Through those Sunday walks, I bequeath
Speaking of which a simple twist of fate
For there's a lot of my father in me

Walking the Coventry canal in the summer
Kicking the grass, chasing the rainbows
And shooting the Indians with sticks
That we would find on the towpath

Friends and family walking in death's line
Dressed in black, mourning the passing
Sitting in their pews singing hymns
Remembering, how we all will miss him

But I recall those halcyon days
Of playing football over the meadows
And, shooting the Indians with sticks.

Kieth Jones

THE SUPER LADY OF MYSTERY

Peggy came in a basket
One Sunday afternoon at tea.
The surprise was most exciting
And realized we now had a member
To go to the land of mystery.
You ran much to the wide open spaces
Only to return to me.
Yes you came back to my whistle
Which you knew immediately.
Your intelligence was most amazing
As you were only a baby really
And we were about to get me into your special car
When you disappeared to the land of mystery.
One day the light will shine
And your eyes will brighten with tears of happiness
And your mystery will be solved.

Silva Stan

THEY

They came again last night I'm sure
sneaked in beneath the bedroom door
Climbed the valance's delicate pleats
and wriggled underneath the sheets

It must have made their pulses pound
the 'thirty-something' flesh they found
'cause up to now I'd won the fight
'gainst creases, wrinkles and cellulite

My 'canvass', so to speak, was bare
devoid was I of underwear
I think though that they chose my face
as an easy 'starting' place

Around my eyes they etched fine lines
(the more obvious of ageing signs)
It looked as if some crows had came
And had themselves a footie game

My boobs were next on the agenda
to see what damage they could render
They pushed and pulled each fleshy mound
till both were nearer to the ground!

Then to my waist these vicious vandals
added flabby white love-handles
A similar curse befell my tum
my hips, my thighs and then my bum

Oh I don't know why on me they prey
expensive lotions won't scare them away
but what really makes me tremble with fright
is wondering what they'll do tonight!

Chris Jones

New Year's Resolution

Old Father Time has been and gone
I heard the old refrain!
It's now two thousand years and one
I welcome with champagne!

My resolution is that I
Won't be the 'weakest link'!
This year my hopes are running high
I should be 'in the pink'!

My first vow then is to be strong
To try to be the best!
I couldn't know before too long
I'd be put to the test!

My second vow is to be wise
And take a wider view
I'll be an angel in disguise
But to myself be true!

My third one is to reach the stars
From Venus I'll hitchhike
Along then comes this man from Mars
Upon his motorbike!

They say that only fools rush in
Where angels fear to ride
But when I dared to take that spin
I felt a sense of pride

For this was not a foolish act
Upon a New Year's night
A challenge had been met in fact
Now I can 'fly my kite'!

Arlene Skerratt

DEEP DOWN

Where sun shines bright on smiling Down,
Where rolling vistas fold,
Where green o'ers green to rocky crown,
That's where my rapture holds.

The sights and perfumes, sounds and stills
Stay never once the same.
Each day, each hour, each minute fills
The heart with joy sublime.

Beneath these scenes and whisp'ring vibes,
Behind this surface charm,
Still further magic truly lies,
Some violent, some calm.

The air we feel but see right through
In frantic movement flies
Of high-speed atoms there's no clue:
There, chaos never dies.

And deeper still when atoms change,
When 'lectrons sudden drop,
The sparks of light sear out to range
Their pathways till they stop.

The search goes on to plumb the depths
Of Nature's secret gifts.
The minds that tease the truth have leapt,
The work they do uplifts.

'Tis said that beauty is skin deep:
That's on the surface true,
But knowledge found gives minds a peep
And shows that beauty's through!

W W Foster

WATER OR LOVE

Water is the heart of life
But is that really so?
Drink a cup of water
Or take my hand tonight?
A few kind words, a caring glance
It's love that's at the heart
Without it
There's no need to drink
You don't want life to last
Without it
You will never smile,
You'll never see the sun
It's love that's at the heart of life
A life that's just begun

A few kind words, a caring glance,
A deed of tenderness
Those smiling lips
The softest kiss
A love so simple and so true
Who needs a cup of water
When all I want is you

Love is the heart of life
But is that really so?
Drink a cup of water
Or take my hand tonight?

Patricia Ferrari

Untitled

I stare at the chair
There's no one there
If only -

Mother's agreed
She's coming to tea
If only

On the shelf sits the clock
Tick-tick-tock
If only.

Hannah arrives
There are stars in her eyes
If only.

I'm deaf you see
And there's no one but me
If only.

Daisy

SUMMER MORN

Once upon a summer morn
We wake to see a new day dawn
The sun appears midst a sky of blue
A variance with rainbow hue

It shows us no mercy, we absorb its rays
This fiery ball of orange haze
And so it is we find ourselves longing
For cooler days

At close of day we see the sun set
As it sinks slowly in the west
The shadows fade, the night grows dimmer
The sun disappears in all its splendour
We let the coolness of the night envelop us.

Phyllis Lorraine Stark

THE TRAMP

A tramp sits all alone
resting on a bench in the sun,
his clothes are ragged and torn
his broken-down shoes badly worn.
The sun shines bright on his grubby old face,
his battered hat shades his eyes,
he seems so restful sitting there
you would think he hadn't a care.
He suddenly gave a rasping cough
as he got up and shuffled away,
he has been ill for most of his life
he appears much worse today.
he's got no money, he hasn't a home
he never knows where he will sleep,
a shelter perhaps or the underground,
or a cardboard box in the street.
On the day he was born he had nothing
and nothing he's had all his days,
so now he waits for the time to come
when he can quietly pass away.

Linda Beavis

Homeless

How did I get here when did it start
When did the happiness start to depart.
I have no address and have no name
People like me are all the same.
I live in the cold and the nights I fear
I ask myself why did I end up here?
Alone on the streets all day long
This is not where I am supposed to belong.

Laura Cannon

IN POLLUTED CITIES LINED WITH MOULD

Septic skies on a windless summer night
Floats above as if it had the right
To take your breath and get under your skin
Tighter, tighter until you're choking.
London coughs and all the while
There's quotes and jokes and perfect smiles
As the yellow cloud sets overhead
Partly toxic, partly lead!
Rats on the ground, rats in the river
Father Thames the ancient sitter.
Vein of truth hide under your buildings
On the banks your mud is gilded.
Human life in meagre dwellings
Blaring music and neighbours yelling.
Baby screaming into the night
And underneath those city street lights
Beautiful London I'm a Londoner divine
Till you're caught on the cesspool of London's wrong side.
When you're caught in the Thames' moon-pulling tide
It's a stark welcome to modern life's landslides.
You're gagging for your best side to get positive
It's all here in London if you really want to live!
Get yourself right up high. Fish yourself out of the deep
Enjoy every single day, until you're swimming in your sleep.
I should turn in, I'm for the worst
But maybe, just maybe I'll write some poetry first!

M J Lloyd

RAILWAY WORLD

I find myself alone in a Starchild world.
I'm just a toy for the Railway Girls.
Once they're bored I am thrown away!
Am I just a game for a Railway Girl?
Starchild dreams burning in the setting sun.
Railway Girls never quite impressed by anyone!

Noel Rainford

STRESS

Everyone these days seems to suffer from stress,
A grand, polite word for your life's in a mess.

Problems may begin, as you get older,
So many troubles for you to shoulder.

The job, if you have one, is not what it was,
And then there's the scourge of the menopause.

If your children leave home, you miss them so much,
Without them around, you feel out of touch.

But then, if they stay, and they won't do their bit,
To keep the house tidy, you wish they would flit.

With parents too, there are changes ahead,
Facing illness or death can fill you with dread.

Being too fat or too thin isn't good for your health,
Same with smoking or drinking and it ruins your wealth.

A kick up the backside won't put these things right,
Nor will swallowing pills help you see the light.

You just have to learn to take it all in your stride.
Sometimes you need help, so forget you have pride.

Learn to accept you are not super-human,
Some things can't be changed, you are merely a woman.

Agnes Cowan

GLACKAPHILIP

The setting was idyllic
Between green fields and blue mountains
Scents of flowers after warm summer showers
Turf smoke and boiling pretties
Powerful unforgettable aromas
Excitement and expectancy of reunited loved ones

There was something else, something indescribable
But as real as dim colour or soft sound
It was the spirit of the place
The countryside was faintly magical even in the rain
Half tones told of it

The soft atmosphere made you feel that you were in
A region that was your proper home
A home that there was neither time nor tide
Or any change at all

Something friendly and akin and full of all that might be needed
If need were to arise, but it never did
For you felt that nothing was lacking
And you did not want to speak

Jim Doherty

LEFT BEHIND

This feeling is overwhelming
Something else is unseen
Forgotten and surpassed
Trodden in our footsteps
Are the dark threads of misery
Concealed among the waste
That forever invades our lives
Unforgiving and regardless
Whether misfortune has been endured
It lays in the dark
Where people never pass
Creeping to and from humanity
In an everlasting battle
That is fought against insanity
Sheltering the fears beneath
Hiding bewilderment from prying eyes
That do so often wander
Where they know they should not

Amy Wragg

MEADOW MAGIC

Sunny, quiet solitude
The rippling brook close by
Stepping stones like glistening pearls
What bliss, indeed, I cry

Violets clumped along the side
Their scent so very sweet
Willows standing there serene
The boughs down to my feet

A little bridge on which to stand
Wood sticks thrown in for fun
Quickly to the other side
To see which stick has won

Daisies all around me
Chains in which to make
Sleeping in the sun above
Such wonders, to awake

Birds are singing softly
So happy with their life
It's a world of true contentment
Without fear and times of strife

No rat-race or a clock to watch
Time enough, for all to share
What beauty to be part of
There is nothing to compare

Reservoir swamps have now replaced
Such beauty, since long gone
However, all my memories
Will forever linger on

Gillian M Ward

SURVIVAL OF THE LUCKIEST

Ecological niches coming and going
Evolution and extinction side by side
An ever changing world
Easing its way through history
Survival of the fittest at all times
Natural selection in all directions
Timescales unthinkable, millions of years
Too long for the mind to make sense of
Dogmatic theories to fit a need
Something missing, something misunderstood.

Catastrophe strikes this Darwinian world
Unsettling systems ingrained in nature
Chaotic patterns disturbed
Extinction after extinction
Calm returns and a species flourishes
A fortunate species
And so here we are
Survival of the luckiest
Now it all makes sense

Tom Sawyer

DEATH'S EXECUTIONER

Waterlogged heaven, a windless sea,
a soundless raven in a leafless tree,
no billowing smoke from the roof does rise,
glass which broke forlornly lies
in empty rooms
bereft of hope.

Darkness looms.

Four gallows stand on a nearby crest
people hang, four abreast -
father, mother, daughter and son,
at their feet another gone -
the family dog
rent open.

Night has come.

Still stand time and nature; in deepest mourning
for that sublime God's creature: Man
Who strives so high
seeking goodness and love -
but the path is too steep!
Instead, tempted by glitter,
he becomes Earth's litter,
offering himself like harvest to reap -

to Death.

So Death visits, taking his due.
And over and over he will reappear,
taking his due.
But leaving the deed of shortening life's span
forever and ever
to man's inhumanity to man.

Clever death!

C M Engler

THE EVACUEE

I'm getting packed,
Ready to go to the country,
I hope that I,
Have a nice family.
I'm packing my teddy,
My gas mask
And my photo too,
I am an evacuee,
I'm going to the country.

I'm at the station,
Clinging to my mum,
I don't want to go,
Won't you come along?
I'm at the station,
I don't want to get onto the train,
Oh, just think of it!
Walking down
A country lane.

I'm at this house,
That I do not know,
I do not like it here,
The wooden beams are so low!
I've got a label,
It makes me so sad,
I'll keep the photo safe,
I wish I never had,
I'm hoping to see Mum,
Down the country lane,
I don't want letters,
I want to see her again!

Rebecca Blackwell

YOUTH REMEMBERED

Oh to be fit enough to run
as I did in the years of my youth
To run on the beach in the pale moonlight
or stride through the wood in the May sun bright
How I enjoyed to stride over moor and fell
or jog through the wood and the quiet dell
To smell the crisp air of a winter's night
or drink the dew of May's first light
Now I watch the world as it passes by
but I will keep my memories until I die.

Wilf Horner

A Private Journey

I despise your words - telling her
who I am, sorting her
something stained.
Words are stupid,
like Reminiscence Day
digging for a cat
buried 20 years.

I'm carrying you.
There, I've built boats of paper filled
with your words,
farcical strangers strewn on deck . . . disconnected
like slaves.

Words floating disentangling
can you hear them? Caressing feet
flooding gardens we built,
to the tree-house the point
where children end,
(a dark stretch).

I adore your silence love
your empty mind. Let's never
use words again. I make you promise

. . . in your sleep.

Neil G Hendry

THE SKY

The soft, warm sky
        as blue as deep cornflower
Gazing into infinite space
Clouds drift by, opaque and airy
An eagle swoops among the vastness
        its shrill cry, echoing the arid landscape
It dips and hovers, swoops and disappears
But still the sky remains

Topaz blue and untouched
It will continue the same
        generation on generation
For all good things never end
        nor do they have a beginning
But continue forward, like time itself.

Shagufta Hussain

SYNCHRONISED SWIMMERS

Fluorescent green sunshine yellow,
covering miles, going nowhere.
Float to top, a fish length apart.
Tail flips a wave, just blowing bubbles.

Cathie Devitt

RIVER!

Gentle flow, winds that blow,
Make the river a nice place to be.
Lap to the shore, for all to adore,
A place for goodness and life.
Time floats by, like a cloud in the sky,
Your mind gets cleared of all thought.
Fishes swim along, the wind plays a song,
Your mind just drifts away.
You sit there and think,
Then it comes to you,
When you're sad,
Come to the river too.

It clears your mind.

Nicole Byrd (13)

WHY

My childhood was without you,
I don't even know your name,
There's a reason why you left me
And I feel I was to blame.
My life is incomplete like emptiness and space,
An identity I've built around a vision of your face.
If you had only seen me, I know that you'd have smiled,
For you'd have seen yourself reflected in the eyes of your own child.

Why was I born if it wasn't your plan,
Will I ever learn who I really am
And why did you leave me, did I make you go?
I was only a baby, how could I know,
Or will I never understand until the day I die,
Why it was you left me and never said goodbye.

Alison Gorton

THE UNIVERSE

What do you do
When your world falls apart?
And everything seems to be
Attacking your heart?
Driving yourself crazy
Feeling so alone
No friend to really talk to
The world fights you on your own.
The people you once knew
Are strangers in a mist
These used to be the people
Who you liked and hugged and kissed.
Unlucky in love
Unlucky full stop
Just waiting for someone else
To take another pop.
Nervous Breakdown Central
Ain't that far away
You're lucky if you can survive
Life just day-to-day.

Lauren Heffer

TIME

Precious moments gone forever,
Forever lost.
Can we afford the cost?

Opportunities, sadly missed,
Missed through stupidity,
Will we ever see?

A bond that's been broken,
Broken beyond repair.
Do we no longer care?

A friendship slowly fading,
Fading into obscurity.
Is this to be our legacy?

True love dying,
Dying before our very eyes.
Is this the prize?

And what my love, tomorrow,
Tomorrow we shall see,
What became of 'you and me'?

Richard Norburn

MARIANA
(Tribute to Tennyson's poem and the Millais painting)

Standing at her window watching
the couples as they go past
her back aches with a certain longing
and the trees stand like empty masts,
shedding confetti upon the lovers.
And the summer now departing . . .
and the leaves will always fall . . .
for the lady who has everything
        and nothing.
Mariana whispers to the wind
'Take my words, oh take my words,
away, away, to him.'

Her lamp is lighted long in the night
but no laughter comes from within.
She stands waiting . . . one day he might
ride in from the north with the only thing
she cannot buy, that will unlock
her face, her heart, her mind.
Then maybe life can begin
for the lady who has everything
        but nothing.
Mariana whispers to the wind
'Take my words, oh take my words,
away, away to him.

She amuses herself from day to day
with her tapestries, with her horses
but as she rides the woods and fields
she often to herself does say
'My life is dreary, he will not come
now the fire of my life is burning away.'

And the light of the day grows dim
around the lady who has everything
       and nothing.
Mariana cries to the wind
'Take my words, please take these words,
away, away, to him.

Guy Moore

THANK YOU FOR YOUR SCRAPS -
I'M A VERY GRATEFUL CHAPPIE

I come here every day to eat up all your crumbs,
I flap my wings and land somewhere and really fill my tum
I leave my mark for all to see, you all know where I've been
I do it all the time dear folks, so unashamedly.
I do it on the statues, on pavements and on walls
And if you let me in your homes, I'd do it in your hall.

It's just my way of saying thank you for the grub.
I don't know any other way, so please don't take the huff.
I'm piling on so much weight though, with gravy, chips and peas.
Go steady on the vinegar too, it makes me want to sneeze.
You really are a messy lot, just dumping things around,
You're lucky that you have me though and all my friends abound.

I love it in the park when school kids sit around.
They laugh and talk and eat and drink and share their little ploys.
They always spill their drinks and leave half of their food
And when I start to help myself, they never think I'm rude.
Office staff come out, the same time every day, they too
Provide much food for me, in fact they make my day.

I love to watch you all, from up there in the sky,
I've really got to know you now, no longer am I shy.
I feel I must complain though, about your dirty ways,
I hate it when you spit on floors and then you urinate.
Why don't you use the toilet, I should talk I know,
But I am just a pigeon, I've nowhere else to go.

I tidy up your cartons and clear your messy crumbs
But climbing through your litter though is really not much fun.
I hate those dirty stumps, the ones that blow out smoke
So many times I've heard you say 'These things just make me choke.'
But still you put them in your mouth, then throw them on the ground
I hate the taste, I hate the smell, I think they're very foul.

Guess what! My wife is pregnant, she told me so today.
I must collect some food for her. I must ward off the prey.
I'm now in such a quandary, perhaps I'll eat for two.
I've got to have some healthy food, I must stay off the booze.
Fresh fruit, salad and vegetables, where will I find these?
No more greasy pies for me and no more mushy peas.

Please have a heart you humans and eat some proper meals.
For I need something healthy now, for my dear Dorothy.
My kids must grow up strong and I must do my best.
I've got to find some wholesome food to take back to the nest.

I know that you can do it, it's really worth a try.
Healthy food is best for all, forget the stodgy pies.
I'll let you know my progress, I'll still leave telling signs.
My family too will thank you all from up there in the sky.

Geraldine Varey

PRESSURE

Clouds hanging over me
Waiting in silence to break,
Nothing to prevent it
It's more than I can take.
The world is on my shoulder
I'm falling to my knees,
Hold my thoughts in a prayer
Help me someone please,
Time can't heal my wounds
It's cutting through my bones,
Too many fires rage
Deep down inside my soul.
To me the world's one room
No windows or with no door,
The pressure is strong and rising
I cannot take much more,
Is this my only destiny?
Is this all I'll ever be?
Will I ever see the day
When happiness belongs to me?

N A Molyneux

LIFE

Where is my God in this world
This day to day living of taking not giving,
And life seen through eyes where vision is blurred.

Will there be just one regret in that moment of truth
With banners upheld and morals rebelled
And man seeking power and eternal youth.

Always the endless disquiet,
The shouting for freedom - oh who will redeem us
From sin and the cold and the dark.

Where is the garden of play
Where children can tumble and laughter's abundant
And little feet skip safely out of harm's way.

Where is my God in this time
Of corruption prevailing depravity, maiming
Honour debated, authority hated and prayer abolished from mind.

The horror of war unrelenting
The innocent pay double-fold,
Oh where is the one heart repenting
Who's saddened by victory's goal.

The riots, the young generation
Are sections we've mapped out alone
But who wins the last big election
When man and his soul are his own.

Roseanne Kelly

TODAY

Yesterday is history
tomorrow is a mystery
the past is the past
and the future won't last.
Yesterday you didn't want it,
today you do and it's gone,
but there's always tomorrow.
The past will last
but the future moves too fast.
Take every chance today
they won't be there every day.
But remember
yesterday is history
tomorrow is a mystery.

Felicity Law

WHAT I BELIEVE

I know what's on your mind.
You want peace and happiness for all on Earth.
But just stop and listen for a moment
To my words for all they are worth.
If there was no suffering
If there was no pain or grief to share
How could you know happiness?
You wouldn't have anything to compare.
You wouldn't know the joy of loving
Someone who meant everything to you
Or you wouldn't appreciate the beauty
Of some lovely scenic view.
How would you recognise the loving look
Of your cat when you tickled her fur
And how would you know she was happy
When you heard her contented purr?
How would you react to music,
Or the sound of laughter in your ears
When you see children happily playing
Because they have no worries or fears?
So you see there has to be some sadness
But nature provides enough of that I find.
So why does there have to be so much cruelty
And suffering caused by the greed of mankind?

Mornee Gill

FELIX VERUS
(or The Real McCat)

What is a cat?

It is the rise and fall of a furry flank,
A leg-of-mutton wash,
A kink in a high-held tail.

It is moments of tension, taut upon the hunt,
Interspersed with long abandonments
To warmth and comfort.

It is a hummock in the eiderdown,
Or a dent in the armchair.
An unwelcome alarm-call at five in the morning.
(Always Saturdays).

It is deaf to command, a sour lump,
That comes unbidden when the heart is tired,
To rub and gaze the hurt away.

A wise soul,
That gives of itself sparingly,
But in true measure.

Philippa Adburgham

BLAME IT ON THE WEATHERMAN

I see, I see, the blind man said.
I know just how he felt.
The shards we walk are sharp and dark the trail of blood.
The pain of happiness an uneasy companion,
It catches you, turns you inside down and upside out.
So bright, so fierce; then asphalt grey.
I know the truth; the truth is easy; we are the truth; we found our truth,
But not the day to day; that is the hurt; the hurt of not.
'We've had the best', and now the rest.
I try to hold it bright and high to know that it is there for me.
Long hours; harsh night and tuneless stars.
I've grazed the sun, now cold is raw, it thrives on the alone.
Separation anxiety; loneliness long distance run.
Is that alone?
We are together, heart, head and spirit, hope and fear; together alone.
Together alone.
The hurt is hard to bear, but harder still the nothing,
Our need is angry, empty arms to fill.
You know my touch, I know your want,
I've held it in my head.
The want is hard, but harder still the nothing.
The path is ours, and ours alone.
We will, we must, we are; we follow where it leads.
So hold us high,
And blame it on the weatherman
When endless clouds sink low.

Peter Wilks

PHOTOGRAPHS

As I stand here by the shore
Taking photos by the score
In this small camera of mine
I am capturing my place in time.

Birds caught in their flight
Fish caught at the bite
Runners frozen at the tape
Cows waiting by the gate.

The white of winter
The green of spring
Even the rain standing still
Suspended there at my will.

Faces of people I have met
In my album they are set
Some pictures are sad, some are happy
Some of a baby in a nappy.

It can be colour or black and white
But still my camera catches the light
Making my memories all come true
Leaving something of me for you.

Kathy Hill

THE SEA

On a calm day,
The boats bob up and down,
There are people playing all around,
The sun sparkles on the sea.

On a stormy day,
The sea is rough,
The boats crash
And the rain falls.

On a calm day,
The sea brings foam,
The small waves go 'Sh',
The people rush to go and surf.

On a rough day,
The waves crash against the rocks
And the waves tower up high
And then they crash down.

Alicia Baker (10)

C'EST LA VIE

She tore through my life and left no trace,
I say her name now with a smirk on my face,
She treated me bad, I was naïve,
I look back now and it's hard to believe,
That was me being played like a fool,
I thought she was fine, I thought she was cool,
I realise now she's a waste of time,
A little girl with men on her mind,
She wasn't that fit, the sex was crap,
I looked at my life and took a step back,
I realised I'd seen this somewhere before,
With one of my friends who was dating a whore,
Everyone said you can do better,
I gave her a chance, I'd only just met her,
They told me to leave her, I could not see,
Blinded by lust, she exploited me,
An experience, it was nothing else,
It could have been worse, I still had my health,
Now it's all over, come to an end,
She wasn't a lover, she wasn't a friend.

Michael Robertson

TO LOVE

In the moonbeams of your eyes,
There my love contented lies,

Away from harm and worldly cares,
You delight with female snares,

I feel protective and sublime,
When our fingers close entwine,

Forever shared, forever blest,
Love is seized at our behest,

We shall never be apart,
Locked - is the chamber of my heart.

A G Trent

THE BUNION

Oh, the pain you're suffering
No one will ever know.
You have a couple of bunions
On the sides of your little toe.

You cannot walk - just hirple
And you're bent in two.
This is really quite awful,
I'm glad that I am not you.

You've had two operations
The relief is great - I know.
The doctors cut and broke your bones
They even shaved your toe!

I know you're now so happy
One thing I want to know.
When you got relief from pain
Where did the spare bits go?

Gillian McNeish

WHAT A DAY

Oh what a day
Things just wouldn't go my way
Each way I looked
There was nothing to say
Oh what a day.

Ann Lacy

THE ONE IN TEN

Who cares about the one in ten?
Not the dole clerk who wields his pen
nonchalantly while calling out 'Next please.'
Not the working man who strives all day
and feels he really earns his pay
while 'idle shirkers' live at their ease.

Who cares about the one in ten?
The boss who cuts the number of men
at his plants feigns social concern.
The theorists can find no answer
to halt this economic cancer.
They fear it will soon be their turn.

Why care about the jobless souls
whose lives lack any structured roles?
They too belong to the human race
who feel sorrow, joy and pain.
Life is more than economic gain;
Each statistic has a human face.

Quintin Douglas

DEATH OF THE RESUSCITATED

I was choking - yet didn't realise,
My eyes were covered by the thick black smoke
And I couldn't see clearly.
It was hot, very hot, in two separate ways.

I thought 'This is it - my time has come,'
But then I was swept off my feet,
By lips that promised
They'd love me forever.

The smoke was getting thicker,
The fire was becoming more intense -
I could feel the heat scorch my neck.
People reached out to help me,
But I was blind and couldn't see.

The fire was ignited by powerful love
With eyes so secretive,
Secretive - I realised then.
Your life was a story,
Full of lies, full of pain.

The fire was extinguished.

I got burnt but didn't die.
The smoke eventually cleared
And once, in a long time,
I saw clearly
And saw the truth.

Michelle Wood

EASTER RISING

Empty tomb and cardboard boxes
Silver foil and linen cloth
Sticky chocolate bloody fingers
Thrusting spear and belly laughs
Mother crying rousing speeches
Piercing lead wooden cross
Healing hands trigger fingers
Hollow shells brown and brass

Eastern setting western rising
Son of God, son of man
Resurrection insurrection
Second coming
First
And last

Oliver Eadie

JUST A TREE

She stands in a field that's evergreen,
The fairest maiden to be seen,
She stands erect and oh so tall,
Much higher than the garden wall.

She lifts her face to the wind and rain
And never once does she complain,
She wears a mantle of green and gold
And never ever will she grow old,
She sways so gently in the breeze,
But after all she's just a tree.

Helen Barwood

You

You are the beauty in a rainbow
You are the calming of the sea
You are the mystery of the stars above
You are what life is meant to be.

You are the dew upon a rosebud
You are the comfort of a home
You are the sunshine after a piercing storm
You are company when I'm alone.

You are the oasis in a desert
You are the flicker of every flame
You are the falling leaf in autumn
You are a crutch when I am lame.

You are the joy of a tiny baby
You are the warmth on a winter's night
You are the eyes of every blind man
You are the reason for every right.

You are the melody in music
You are the moral in every line
You are the reason for all living
You are everything, you are mine.

Debbie Taylor

LIFE HISTORY

A child throughout the fifties, I did as I was told,
Showing deference to grown-ups, who all seemed very old.
A teenager I then became before they'd quite begun,
Rock 'n' roll and sex and drugs weren't quite our kind of fun.
The cinema, then home by ten, not partying all night
And a quick kiss on the doorstep in the glare of the porch light.
But finally at twenty-one they let me have a key,
At last, I thought, a chance to have some fun and to be free.

But I married Someone Sensible whose prospects seemed quite good
And we bought a little semi, just north of Cricklewood.
And then we had a daughter, followed quickly by a son,
The busy years of parenthood had really now begun.
No time to think of what I'd like or who I want to be,
Nor any cash for anything at all to do with me.
It's not that I'm complaining, but it doesn't quite seem fair,
There's fun and good times to be had and I would like a share.

But children grow up pretty fast and soon they're leaving home,
One's off to study medicine and one the world to roam.
My chance has come at last I think . . . but wait, now Granny's old,
She wants to come and live with us and her house must be sold.
But life goes round in circles and it's never as you think,
For Granny likes to run the home, tied to the kitchen sink.
At last I have some freedom and life's an open door
And I'm off to university at the age of fifty-four.

Mary Barville

LOVE

within its embrace
the world stands still
framed in this equator
of arms

overhead, the word
the glowing angel with book-like
hands, proclaims from the spheres
that we are one
world

standing on the Seine, unsinking
the Eiffel offers us bouquets
of leaves
we have no interest for them
nor for the moons and stars
that fall
about us

I bow my head into your soul
hoping your arms
are strong enough
to hold and circle
this fragile voyage

Kirsten Kearney

BREAKING THROUGH

It's cold on my skin this fiery wind,
Blowing up and around,
I've caught a chill and lost my will,
Blowing down and around,
My mind won't start - it follows my heart,
Breaking up and around,
My spirit feels cheap in my life so bleak,
Breaking down and around,

There's this sound I hear as the wind tells tears,
Tearing through my town,
But a blackbird is silent as the wind is violent,
Tearing on my face my frown,
So I go to the tree that gave birth to me,
Trying to gain ground,
But the blackbird lands on my tree's warm hands,
Trying to spite my ground,

All of a spark - a fire in my heart,
And the sun stains the ground,
The tree comes to life uprooting my strife
And blackbird makes an awful sound,
I'm getting warm as I'm bringing my storm,
My spirit has found its crown,
And my cruel wind is blown and my frown is thrown,
My tree stands tall in my ground.

C J Hatherall

THE SEVEN SISTERS

Minute algae
bathing luxuriously
in sub-tropical water
calcareous
hardening
on the sea-bed
invisible crusting
for thirty million years
until the sea,
cooling,
withdraws,
liberating the shapes
of sibling nymphs
huge and voluptuous
who have bided their time.

Glorious in sunlight
their white bones
beckon,
graveyard for algae
and sailors,
the difficult sea passage
reminding us
that whatever we control
it is not this.

Lynda Morgan

HOPE

We all hope for something,
at some time in our life.
Be it health, wealth or happiness
and that we'll be free from strife.

No more wars, but peace on earth
and in harmony we will live.
Hopefully all the hungry
will be fed by those who give.

We hope for all the lonely
in their darkest hour.
That God will give them comfort
if it's within his power.

The young men of destruction
may they learn there is no gain.
The troubled and the suffering
be released from all their pain.

Let's hope our children's future
improves beyond compare.
Our dreams seem unattainable,
but we'll survive while hope is there.

Mona Brown

THE DEER

The sun beats down,
The sky is clear,
Nothing stirs,
But a soulful deer.

The wood is cool,
A breeze through the grass,
The deer is alert
With eyes like glass.

He skips through the trees
Silent and soft,
Down by the lake,
On a carpet of moss.

A few sips of water
He raises his head,
A pheasant takes flight,
The deer has fled.

He returns to the meadow
Enjoying the sun,
Bouncing over streams,
But he knows they will come.

Shaun Nash

LANGUAGE CLASS

We sit, English lips
moving in a most un-English way,
babbling child-like
in front of university graduates;
our mouths mouth sounds
which are a shade too labial
or dental, or nasal,
but the nuances are lost
on graduates, no matter how bright
or formal; the native foreigner
at his side
will soon dispel moot points.
Learned at his mother's knee
they are not even academic
but just well-known and loved
expressions of his other land.
But we hug our new-found
symbols to ourselves;
these secret sounds are ours
if we can but remember them.
And if our lips are moved
within the narrow limits
imposed by long usage,
we can bring a smile
to the face of a Spaniard
or Turk, can argue with an
irate Italian or undo
the puzzle-lock of Linear-B.

L Saunders

FEEDING RABBITS

Each day near dusk
the old man takes the hessian sack
and seeks out the soft armpits of the field
where the dandelion grows
each clump a solar system
served by its yellow suns
burns brighter in the darkening grass
as birdcall slows
and leaves this great creaking wheel to the corncrate

Pluck them not says folklore
these despised p***-the-beds
that stand firm and defiant on translucent tubes
ignoring the wind as if to mock nature

He raises the rusty hook
its edge a fearsome shine from the carborundum
and decapitates the flower and massacres the heavy-
veined leaf
spilling its coming white blood
and fills the sack until it smells
of some recently-sired animal

Then slowly he moves up the breast of the hill
quivers a moment on the skyline and disappears
with the sun under his oxter.

Wilson John Haire

I WONDER WHY

I wonder why the sad things in life are often free,
I wonder why the world can't love, to do so is easy,
to understand the feelings, numb, yet without sharing,
it would be such a better place to have a little caring,
to be left in a crowded room, can still bring loneliness,
to have, to hold, to cuddle up, a little soft caress,
my life has been a battle, as long as I can think,
yet when I think about it, I can read it in a blink,
but life is so precious, and to think 'I wonder why?'
will only knock you down a step an make you once more cry.
Life is like a ladder, there's two ways you can go,
at the bottom, at the top or may be to and fro,
so when you're hard done by, you want to sit and cry,
remember all the ones worse off, who want nothing else but die.
The pain inside the head, is worse than a heavy blow,
If you feel that this is it, good luck it's time to go,
no goodbyes should dare be said, just a simple bye,
maybe it would be different if I didn't wonder why.

Lynne Richardson

PLASTIC VESICLE

I am a cup
drip
first empty
drip
unused
drip
uncomplicated
Fill me with your consequence
drip
your falsity
Your distortion and deception
Like a waxen vase I stand dormant
Holding
drip
your thick complex solution
Until you selfishly
drip
fill me
You don't stop
drip
I am bursting
drip
swelling
drip
spilling
You tumble out of control sapping my structure
drip
engulfing me
Then
drip
nothing
full
drip
but not filling

Then
drip
you drain me ingesting what flooded me and more until my cold base shows
Then you leave me in the dark
Standing alone empty useless still waiting
As quiet as a cup
No flow simply an inconsistent drip
Until
drip
a spider drops and weaves its dry net
Closing me
Inhabitable but unusable
I fester and taint
You forget

Laura Holt

THE COUNTRY LANE

As I walked down a country lane
One beautiful summer day
I heard the birds a singing
As I went on my way

A mistle thrush flew from a hedge
A robin sang in a tree
A little owl sat on a fence
And seemed to be watching me

I stopped to look at bluebells
Red campion as well
And on the breeze I caught a sniff
Of their beautiful smell

A timid rabbit watched me
From among the grass
I tried not to scare it
As I carefully went past

On my way home I saw a stoat
A lizard and a shrew
And as I went on walking
The lane was lost from view

And as I went to bed that night
I thought about the lane
And when the sun is out once more
I shall go there again.

Vanessa Bell

THEODOLITE TERROR

Sounds of passion
from behind the privets
primeval three-legged monsters
emerge to barks of assent
from frightened poodles
Are they alive?
the people ask
as these creatures
begin to colonise
this sleepy small town setting
They inflict their
imperial culture
on the non-consenting masses
Systematic savagery
in the pursuit of progress
scandalises
the terrace-dwelling tv age
townsfolk
They fight a ferocious
rearguard action
but for this backyard
of Britannia
the day of the theodolite
has dawned

John Williams

MY PRIMROSE

My love grows by the wayside,
Amid the grasses, now she lies.
No sound, no whispers.
She hides.
Beautiful perfection,
She gives a perfumed sigh,
Come the springtime
Born again carpeting the woodlands
In her green and yellow dress
There grows my sweetheart, my love,
So named she lives
Again my darling sweet Primrose.

V N King

A Melody Of Sound

I heard a golden melody like choirs of angels singing
The sound of many voices within my head was ringing
The sound I heard as so elusive as I tried to find the source
Of that sweet and heavenly music that filled my heart with so much force
I heard the harp so pure and clear, a voice with soaring note
The sweetness of the sound I heard caused an ache within my throat
Alas it was only in my dreams, a fantasy did make
If only I could hold those dreams to keep with me when I awake.

Dorothy Irvine

CAT LOVE

She sits there in all her majesty
She's queen of her domain
Nothing ever ruffles her
Come snow or wind or rain.
I know her eyes are following me
As I walk out of the room
Those beautiful emerald eyes of hers
Which seem to say come back soon.

She has been for a stroll
Round the garden
And flattered my catmint bed,
Had an argument with her friend next door
Though little was said.
Now she sits by the kitchen door
Waiting to be fed
And looks at me with those beautiful eyes
And nothing needs to be said.

For she knows that I will oblige her
Whatever her wants may be.
For the state of her composure
Is because she has faith in me.
She knows that whatever she asks of me
I will do with pleasure
And as you have guessed, I love my cat
She is my greatest treasure.

Vera Jones

ALBORADA

I had two dreams
Of a girl with green skin.
She had silver on her hands,
And memories within.

She's a green-skinned baby,
Holds the scents of temples in her hands.
She wears the beads of generations 'round her wrists,
And gold and silver charms adorn her.

She told of how things tasted on the shore.
She sang of wasted days in Asia.
She poised her endless graces
Like a hundred dreams of love.

And in another dream she danced an *alborada;*
Tied her hair,
Wrapped her hair in linen,
Oiled her feet before she stepped into the sun.

Her dance is measured and exacted,
Her darkest moments re-enacted.

Steps in shadow when she dances.

Olive Yates

MISS YOU

I cried myself to sleep last night
A vision of Mum would not come to sight
If I can't see her, how will I remember
Will her memory fade like the last burning ember
I found her photo and I felt so much better
I wanted to tell her, to phone her, to send her a letter

Who will I talk to now that she has gone
No one can replace her for she was the one . . .
Who knew how I felt without having to tell
She made me feel better, though she was not well

I try to remember the good times and the laughter we shared
I hoped she knew I loved her, how much I really cared
I never used to tell, when I used to phone
And now that she's not there, I feel all alone

I know I've got my family and they're very dear to me
But who will be my Mum now that she's not here for me
That must sound selfish for I know she's free from pain
But a part of me is missing until I see her once again

Today the girls placed Mum's ashes upon her Mum's grave
They planted lots of pansies and both were very brave
Carol cried as usual but they also laughed some too
Especially when the rain came and soaked them both right thru

Mel said it was a sign from Mum because Carol had complained
That the pansies were too dry and that is why it rained
So although I cannot see her I know that she is here
She sends us little signs, so we won't live in fear
For one day we will see her and hold her once again
In a place of no regrets, no sadness and no pain.

Angie Wheeler

FORBIDDEN WHISPER

Having lived and lost
I find my love reserved.
No longer young freedoms in this old embrace.
My time is torn it seems,
And yet such speed, such haste.
The head speaks of caution for the ready love,
the heart, still reeling from the foolish move,
races unknowingly.
Oh forbid that the two should ever mix
or the two should whisper in dark corners:
such secrets as pain never saw.
Sweet quiet would find a ready home here
to mingle its softly spell.

Richard Oliff

IN MEMORIAM

'No flowers please. Donations to the Cats Protection League are welcome.'

My Mum had a soft spot for a pussy-cat,
And the League that protects them from this and that,
So it seemed just purr-fect, and would suit us well
To channel all gifts to the CPL.

Maybe I should have smelt a rat
When I asked, 'How will this gift help pussy-cat?'
Well, you should have seen me suddenly blanch
When they said, 'We'll buy pens for every branch.'

I didn't know whether to cry or laugh -
'What! Spend it on biros for all the staff?'
But then I turned pink from ear to chin . . .
The 'pens' were just *cages,* to keep moggies in!

David Wilson

THE PRECINCT IS NEAT

The precinct is clean, the precinct is neat,
Except for leaves that fall just now.

The texture of leaves is yielding and warm,
Shapes of leaves are exotic and curved,
The colour of leaves is startling, but right.

The fall of the leaves is quiet and soft,
But the precinct is neat,
It's lines are all straight
To keep noises of feet,
For the shoppers who wait.

Now, leaves are like letters of love,
From the tree to the earth,
'Thank you brown earth,
for giving me birth,
The winter is coming
And I will be cold,
Please do sustain me,
My leaves love and hold'

'Yes I'll take your leaves
And warm up your feet;
Until you grow more
To save you from heat,
When summer comes . . .
And the precinct is neat.'

Peter Henry

KNOWING IS WITHIN

We seek and question
Ask the neighbours
A friend
Mother or father
Son or daughter
Often a complete stranger
Knowing is within

Decisions, decisions
Must be made
But not today
I'll ask my neighbour
Friend, mother or father
Son or daughter
And possibly a stranger
Knowing is within

When the gut twinges
Nerves jangle
Sweat trickles
The answer's no!
No need to question
My friend
Knowing is within

When there is stillness
Peaceful serenity and calm
The answer is yes!
No need to question
My friend
Knowing is within

The sadness of
Wrong decisions
Based on asking the neighbour,
Friend, mother and father
Son and daughter
And even a stranger
Knowing is within.

Jude Le Sage

A Little Word

May I have a word in your ear?
About something I would like to make clear
I tell you darling from my heart
I feel we will never part
You and me we really suit
Although at first - you was forbidden fruit
I hoped my feelings were not wrong
We were right for each other all along
We used to smoke a little hash
And occasionally blow our cash
But now our lives have rearranged
And the course we took has changed
Noticing it was doing harm
We both sat up - heard the alarms
It really would have been a shame
If our lives had stayed the same
So to give some assistance
We gave that world some distance
And now we have left this world behind
The lessons learnt - still in our minds
And so to continue with my story
I'll tell of our lives, our glory
Both have had loves that came and went
And many of our years have been spent
Waiting for that honest love
That fits together like a hand in a glove
Rebuilding our hearts at a pace
Craved a soulmate - unhappy with the space
Though we have travelled loads
I know between us . . . we have learnt loads.

Pam Spencer

IF I WON THE LOTTERY

I'm just a slip of a lass
If I won the lottery
Think of all the brass
Yet to me a fortune to hold,
That lovely warm feeling,
In from the cold.
What to buy and try,
Lots of lovely things to do.
No more money worries again,
Good times, and men.
Just think I'd be able to buy that
Horse and stable, the car, the house and
The swimming pool.
I'd be sensible, with the money,
And not play the fool.
A lottery win provides wealth,
But one thing, that is also a richness, is to have
Good health.

Caroline Janney

TICKING CLOCK

Tic toc tic toc
So runs the clock
Ticking, ticking the time away
Tic toc tic toc

Today begets tomorrow
Tic toc tic toc
Tomorrow scents the day to follow
Tic toc tic toc

The clock cares not
When winding is forgot
Batteries wear out
Electricity goes berserk.

But somewhere
Always runs a clock
Ticking our lives away
Tic toc tic toc.

Seconds turn to minutes
Minutes become hours
Hours bring nights
Followed by days.

Days switch to months
Months to years.
Just that ticking clock
Adds years to years to years.

To make us all
Older and older and older
Why not kick that ticking clock
Tic toc tic toc tic toc.

Ruth Brigden

HOW TIMES CHANGE

At the entrance, to the park
I sit in the car, but hear no lark
Up high, and I wonder why?
The grand-children, are busy at their play
As always, forever and a day.
Isn't it strange, how we walk our dogs,
Nobody takes them, when they jog.
No time-honoured walk, down to the park
Now, now, they are taken in the car.
They jump out of the back of the car
For, they soon know where they are.
Glad to get out of the confines of home
From which, they would never, ever, roam
For they know when, they're well off!
Alsations, black Labradors, and the Westies,
Are people's companions, whatever the seasons.
With big towels, some are wiped down
Especially, when there's wet mud to be found.
To keep the car clean, and in good shape
Even though, the dog's paws, must ache.
But they seem to enjoy, their annual walk
Would they tell us, if they could talk?
To be out in the clean fresh air, and the lovely smells,
In the air, of the countryside
I wonder, just look at the dog's eyes, they'll let you know
How much they enjoy, where they go, to sniff the grass, and
Walk the path, of their ancestors?

Rosemary Peach

MOVING DAY

When you picked the flat you could have told me that
    It was three flights up in the air
    Although it's not unique
    It's tough on yer feet
And it don't help it's in the middle of Ware

Breath you begin to lack
You have an asthma attack
You're hanging on to the wall
Your will begins to crack
When you see the furniture stack
Next time you move, don't call.

Terry Rogers

SCHOOL

What horrible person invented schools?
And who invented all those rules?
In school why do we have to think?
And why can't uniform be bright pink?
We have to read boring books
And if we talk we get bad looks.
Why is school invented at all?
I'd rather run into a brick wall!
And then they make us do those sums
And we can't even eat chewing gum!
What horrible person invented schools?
And who invented all those rules?

Sophie Levi (11)

THE BIRTH

A miracle of life, a union of love
Innocent and pure, a gift from above
Thrust into a world from a loving entomb
First cries of protest will surely come soon

Each second a lifetime the silence heartfelt
This struggle for life no one can help
All eyes shine with hope for the first feeble sign
Praying with fervour against passing of time

Oblivious to all little fists flay and curl
Each cry is such music, joyful to all
Each movement a wonder, enchanting to see
This miracle of life living and free.

Mary O'Hara

AUTUMN

Crisp and sharp winds do blow
Scrunch and crunch the leaves go
As I walk a calm and slow pace
In the forest at autumn, such a
                beautiful place.

Colours so many and all do blend
Autumn is not sad, not seasons end
Just making way for winter's turn
So spring can arrive, new life
                can be born.

Enjoy each season to the full
Each one brings its own rewards
The beauty of autumn, lovely bird calls
It is all to amazing for simple words.

Sallyanne Hayes

THE LOCK KEEPER

Heat beating down. Heat beating.
Fired tongues scorch earth's creatures
and greenery and growth tumble
untidily down and down
along the uneven river's edge.
Frothed waters carry life's detritus.
Broken branches - a deluge from chaotic flood
whirl in a maelstrom of locked waters.

Nettles fight angrily along a marked pilgrim's path,
grasping towards blue, unbroken sky.
Vice-like they bite marked flesh -
a serpent's kiss hidden in an undergrowth
of lost paradise.

Three pilgrim travellers halt abruptly and wait . . .
The black and white colossus straddles
still, murky waters.
An awesome obstacle to their path.
Progress halted. Journey interrupted.
Pause . . . Breath . . . Stillness . . .
Heat beating down. Heat beating.
And in a moment, in one dancing breath of time
his spirit hovered on the waters.
The honeyed bee buzzed harmoniously
and amongst the shrill crescendo of birdsong
the soft ascendance of an insect
carried humble thoughts upwards.

Silence imposed. Journey halted. Silence surrounds.
Soft mutterings of desire rise slowly on the breath of the afternoon.

The lock keeper imperceptible, forceful
guides the pilgrim three.
Colossal gates invite an entrance,
swallowing small boat within a cavernous mouth.
Raging waters are soothed and calmed.

Slowly, silently, grace, not sought, is given and bestowed.
In one dancing breath of time, thoughts rise upwards,
we rise upwards
towards the bulking figure of the lock keeper.
And powerless to provide our own direction
we rejoice in his quiet, controlling force
pointing us onward.

G R McCauley

DARK OF NIGHT

Rainbows, above canopy covered four poster beds,
unicorns, with solitary ivory horns on their heads.
Smiling, laughing clowns, memories of lovers,
good times spent, with fathers and mothers.
Peace, serenity, a fabulous feeling of floating,
like being covered by a cotton wool coating.
Shining armoured knights, damsels in distress,
fairy tale endings, silk and satin wedding dress.

Perfect utopia, ideal individually created world,
where, in the land of nod, you find yourself hurled.
Headlong, meeting landscapes, mesmerising visions,
creations of mind and reality, with no divisions.
No malevolent nightmares, disturbing your sleep,
just a perfect night, in a dream, superbly deep.

In the dark of night, inside your mind,
scenes like these, I hope you'll find.

Inspired by the birth of a young lady, Nuala.

Danny Coleman

A Happy Question

Why is it that all those who pray
With Christian fervour each day
Are not so endearing
As those who are veering
To sin, as they travel life's way?

E M MacLennan

SIC ITER AD ASTRA
(SUCH IS THE WAY TO THE STARS)

In man's quest to reach the stars
there is a price that some must bear
and danger ever present demands utmost care
for the worst can sometimes happen
with great engines of fire
and all will hold their breath lest
they see a funeral pyre.

On January 17 in nineteen sixty seven
three calm and valiant men were at the
gates of heaven
sitting in 'Apollo' on a rocket
Saturn One B
in an atmosphere of oxygen as volatile
such a gas can be.
With cruel perversity of fate the exercise
was blighted
for a deadly spark was present and the gas
became ignited.
In less than twenty seconds the worst
tragedy realised,
the astronauts had died beneath the
darkening skies.

Tom Crean

UNTITLED

A darkened room, heavily curtained
Masking the external gleam
And dimming his internal glow

His frail and fragile body
Once abundant with strength, moving fast
Now depleted and slow

His dwelling was bright, scented and warm
Until the cold seeped in
And the winds did blow

There she laid so limp and cold
Then rigid and grey
With these tidings he reached his low

Withdrawn and withered
His life has no meaning and thinking
Of his loss brings such woe

Nourishment lacking, his skin looks so pale
Almost translucent as he mourns
With such sorrow

A skeletal figure lays in a tranquil position
Grasping a yellowed image
Of whom he will follow

From his plot in the parlour
An exhausted final sigh departs this sedate cadaver
A gift that only God could bestow

An immense sense of delight and relief elevated his soul
A reunion with his beloved
Which would surely grow

Jaime-Louise Holmes

UNTITLED

The world is upside down it seems,
and man has failed in all his dreams
of universal wealth and peace,
equality that will not cease.

The wealth we have in part at least;
one third enjoy a daily feast.
But happiness, the common good -
these things are rarely understood.

The world is splitting at the seams,
and every town and city teems
with unplanned children, who will move
through life without the taste of love.

Yet there are others who know death
before they even draw first breath.
Or those whose lives will foully end
in war, as man strikes out at friend.

The future looms oppressed and dark -
man's selfishness has left its mark,
and we have little left to give
our children's children, should they live.

But if, before it is too late
we can attempt to halt the hate
and sadnesses, then we just could
begin to turn our world towards good.

Helen Setchfield

NORTHERN LIGHTS

Desperately ecstatic tonight,
I want to light
       your sky
So brilliantly,
But there!
I am weighted
By the heavy tread
Of feuding doubt.

Effortlessly
       Bi-polar,
I can hang onto a fluffy cloud,
Or drop like a stone
Into a murky pond
Of sullied experience -
       Hang on tight,
       And we might catch
       A northern star
       Before it turns
             to ice.

Joy Thorpe

THE RACING PIGEON

When I was a squeaker in the nest with my mate
My registration ring was placed on my leg before it was too late.

Learning to fly from my loft to explore is a major factor
My first serious mistake can be a real disaster.

Training is designed to help me be my own companion
Following others will not make me a champion.

Plenty of rich variation in my diet provides my energy
Exercise not dietary is the key to successful husbandry.

Watching the early sun rise aids my orientation
I must be quickly away to be first to my destination.

Wires and birds of prey are a reality
Careful observation will lead me to my sanctuary.

My superior racing genes are held in perpetuation
By selective breeding and planned propagation.

My ancestors crossed the Channel many times as part of the strife
To carry secret war messages to try and save life

Many hours of non-stop flying shows my determination
Racing pigeon fanciers world-wide display their admiration.

Brian Bates

FLECKS OF RAIN ON MY FACE

Before the short journey
to the cold, sterile place of farewell,
I see dew on our secret rose
like a tear-filled eye.
Now is no time to empty
my heart to it.

I note the misted flowers
I can't bear to cut.
The grass is a damp cushion and
the pines like wet umbrellas.
The wind flaps skirt-like and
the river tinkles like wind chimes.

The hand-built, black conveyance
waits at the gate for her this morning.
In my heart a cold, blue candle burns,
straining to shine bright while
the wind gusts the first, cold
flecks of rain on my face.

Keith Lobban

WIDOW'S SON

Look at the widow's son
Look at the great job that she has done
Put aside her fear and grief
Rules she applied, but she was brief

Hiding her hurt and pain until the night
She wanted her son's future look bright.
She lives on her memories by day and by night.
Surely it keeps away the fright.

Constantly watching her son's good deeds
Every hour in the day she's there for his needs
He's grown up now, he's been given a wife
It'll keep him out of trouble and strife
His weekend visits go longer and longer
That's good he and his wife will get stronger.

I pray every night to God above
To reunite me with my love
I've sent my son off, he has wed
Please Lord let me die in my bed.

I'm with my love, time's endless now
This Lord that, you did vow
We'll watch over you our son
You're our baby, our only one.

Seorsé De Sansaim

THE TALE OF MR SMITHERS

One day a little badger came and laid outside my door
It looked so sad and hungry and had blood on its paw
The badger was so wet and cold and needed to get rest
I'd never nursed a badger but I'm sure I'd do my best.

He must have weighed 3 stone or more but still he looked so small
His eyes were glazed and nose was dry, his ears they were so sore
I thought he must have had a fight but not with one the same
He'd come across some poachers out looking for their game.

My friend the little badger was soon up and well again
Not knowing that his home had gone and colony at its end
His curiousness, it made me laugh when he met my dog called Molly
He wasn't sure of her wagging tail and tongue that felt like jelly.

He'd bark when he was hungry and sleep when he was tired
He'd tug and pull for a bit of fuss whenever he desired
With his fur as black as coal dust and stripe as white as white
He'd go off for more adventure in the middle of the night.

One day my little badger had been gone a day or more
I thought he'd met the poacher and he'd settled the score
My worries were soon over as my badger did come home
I think he'd found a family but still he was alone.

I named my little badger when he'd lived with me a while
I named him Mr Smithers, he would always make me smile
He brought alot of joy to my life and Molly he did too
I hope my tale of Mr Smithers has brought some joy to you.

Cherrylyne

FATHER

A big strong man
With a heart of gold
Never a cross word
Never a groan
A gentler man you could not meet
For me there is no other

For you are the man that I looked up to
And you guided me in ways
That brought me from this child
To the woman I am today.

Thanks Dad!

Helen McAlinden

AN AUDIENCE OF COOKS

There was a cheeky young lady called May Belline
I said to her, you look so terrible
Like nothing I've ever seen.
She had long hair and glasses to hide her face
I said, I'm not surprised
She had factor forty on her face.
I said, do you know my friend?
His name is Max Factor
Max Factor, she said, that terrible actor.
I said, do you not know him?
He's a very famous painter
Yeah, he paints women's faces
To make them look pretty and younger.
I said, how old are you?
You must be about twenty-one
But you'll look like a model
When your horrible make-up has gone.
I said, do you know a woman called Mrs A Von?
Who, she said, does she dress like a man?
I laughed but said no, she works in Boots
But you should see her looks.
I said, do you know what beauty is?
It's skin deep
The young lady of six said, do you know what a cliff top is?
It's more than nine feet.
I said, do you know what a mirror is?
It reflects your looks
She said, do you know who my father is?
He's one of those mad cooks.

N Donaldson

DO YOU BELIEVE IN GOD?

Do you believe in God?
How many really do?
When you look around
It appears only a few.
But we all have our ways
Of following our faith,
Some say their prayers
Just to play safe.
Others keep it to themselves
Close to their heart,
Showing how they feel
That's the difficult part.
Your God is your God
No matter who you are,
Whether you show your feelings
Or worship from afar.
Whatever your preference
It matters not a lot,
Because we are seen as equal
In the eyes of God!

Derek Pile

CHARLIE

Isn't science wonderful!
Charlie is a robot, he has been with me
Ever since poor Mrs Ponsonby
Was found
        mangled and strangled
        and dead in her bed

Isn't science wonderful!
He thinks like a human, he's always so cheerful,
Of course there's no need to be fearful,
I know it's easy
        to feel queasy
But, today, my pint of beer
        tasted queer.

Advertisement as follows:
Owing to employer suddenly expiring
Experienced robot is requiring
Responsible position
        on condition
        it must
Be one of absolute trust . . .

Joanna Carr

EXIT TO HEAVEN

I knocked on the door to heaven
and waited for a reply
hoping to be admitted
to this place where you go when you die.
'Who dares knock upon my door?'
A deep growling voice replied
'Why it is me,' I said meekly
'My name is Fred Clough,
and I've come from the other side.'
'Are you dead?' the voice asked,
'Or just dreaming?'
'I hope you're not wasting my time,
can you name the funeral director,
who's a passing acquaintance of mine.'
I thought long and hard of his question,
what idiot would ask me of this
then my thoughts clicked in place
as I lay in a daze.
It was the Devil taking the mickey!

R Burk

IT'S TIME TO GO

Lying in my bed
Thinking of friends and relatives
Of times past, both happy and sad
Moaning, groaning in agony
Crying tears, full of pain
Receiving tender loving care
From people who genuinely care
Feeding, changing, tucking-in
Receiving injections and pills regularly
Always heavily drugged
Days never ending
Nights are never there
Visitors call but never stay
Some a few minutes, a few a couple of hours
I wish they would go away
But I want them here and near

Sun shines, snow falls
Rain drizzles, wind howls
Green fields, perfumed flowers galore
Trees and shrubs
Dogs barking, cats mewing
Sheet bleating, cattle lowing
Birds in flight, singing their song
Sons and daughters, their spouses and children
I'll miss them all

I hear my name from afar
God is calling - *it's time to go!*

Margaret Monaghan

CALEDONIA

In bonnie Scotland
we have heather and stones
for our breakfast
and deep fried Mars bars
for tea
yes, it's great to live here
we fight and argue all day
for we are an argumentative
disputatious race
wee hard men
with red hair drinking buckfast
giving each other
the Glasgow kiss
are you staring?
are you looking at me pall?

Glasgow girls
have greasy thick lips
Glasgow girls like their fish and chips
most of the people
you see
wearing kilts
are Americans
and public school boys
I do love to see
the midges biting the tourists
it's not nice
I know
but sometimes you
can't move for them
the bloody tourists I mean

Julian Ronay

THE GREEN AND PLEASANT VALLEY

Hawes is one of the main centres of the Yorkshire Dales and Gayle is the little village satellite which clusters like a suburb around the rushing waters of a tributary as it gushes in great force down the slopes of the adjacent Dodd Fell that reaches over two thousand feet in the vicinity of the village, on its way into Wensleydale.

The Hawes region is the main village of Wensleydale, along which flows the River Ure. The Pennine Way passes by both Gayle and Hawes, the latter becoming very crowded with visitors during the summer months, particularly on market days.

When I arrived in Hawes, having walked all the way from Skipton, Gayle was the first village I came to. It was evening and the narrow, cottage-lined footpath echoed with the sound of my tramping feet, my back heavily laden with tent and ruck sack. Those cottages, facing one another across this narrow, twisting pathway, so narrow that you could almost reach out and touch each opposite wall, seemed very ancient and crumbling, a throwback to a different time and very eerie in the growing twilight.

Then I dropped into Hawes and camped the night. In the morning I took the bus into Richmond, following the River Ure along Wensleydale. Then from Richmond, I took the bus up Swalesdale to Keld where I resumed walking along the Pennine Way, all the way to High Force in Teesdale. But those first glimpses of Gayle stand out in my memory because as I arrived at the bridge over the thunderous river, shirt-sleeved locals were out taking the evening air, relaxing in the sunshine and it really did, in those days, seem like a different world.

P Loudon

MY LIFE

This is my life to live,
And no one's but my own,
This is my life to live,
From the seed that you have sown,
Let me rise with my achievements,
Watch me fall with my mistakes,
Let me face all of its challenges
To find out what it takes,
How will you judge if I succeed,
By my prosperity and wealth,
I would ask that you look first,
At my happiness and health,
Let me suffer all its heartaches,
Let me absorb all the joy,
Whatever happens on my journey,
I will always be your boy,
Fill me with your knowledge,
Before you set me free,
Take comfort in the fact,
That you travel on with me.

D Woodford

MILLENNIUM

The new Millennium is coming
  And with it changes all around,
They say computers will all crash
  If a solution isn't found.

I'm afraid I do not understand
  How a computer knows the date,
Will they not just carry on
  Or will the world be in a state?

Why wasn't this all thought out
  In the many years that have past,
Has man only thought of today
  And how to make money fast?

The year 2000 is a short way off
  When all machines will be put to the test,
It really all should work out fine
  If man has done his very best.

Ann Ogilvie

THE COTTAGE WOODEND

Over the moors, stark and lonely
And where one sees for miles around
As the car makes its journey
Through unending ups and downs
And leaving behind the busy towns
This is real, the wonderful green
Of the countryside in Teesdale,
As on our way we go to the cottage
This a very special place hidden away.
At the top of a hill, very private
You open the gate and drive through
Shutting it safely behind you,
And there it is, a place of rest
With beauty all around
Tucked away so no-one can find you
A little bit of heaven
In this crazy world today.

Johanna Nicoll

OLD LOVER'S LAMENT

I didn't make much of my life.
I hope you made more of yours,
But then I know where you're living . . .
We're just distant people, on distant planets,
Too far to ever touch, so close we meant so much.
So living in a dream wasn't much your scene,
Then it wasn't mine,
But it was all I had to offer
And if the dream didn't come true,
It still can't be a lie, if we didn't even try,
And I guess we never tried.
So we cut our losses
And you got married
Then I got married
And cut my losses
And for a while, I had to smile.
Oh, I've been happy
And I've been sad
And I've taken pleasure from people I should never had.
But when I can't sleep,
And I'm thinking of someone deep
I still think of you
And all of those might have beens
But I suppose no one ever wins
On a good day we waste our time
And when it's bad we waste our minds.
So why would I wish to waste your time
When this love's not yours anymore, but mine.

K D Lloyd

ACCIDENT

Oh God! Why doesn't she stop screaming?
Crouching on the floor, retching over the stained white bowl.
Can't somebody stop her screaming?
I want to be sick, let me get rid of this feeling of disgust.
Closing the windows won't shut out the screams of pain
That even all the pillows on my bed won't deaden.
Please let me be sick and stop this awful noise.

The screech of brakes, followed by the breaking glass,
And the sickly thud of a human body.
The moments silence, then the shouts of passers-by,
And the screaming starts.
'God he's hit them!'
'I think she's dead!'
'Where's the phone?'
'Two little girls!'
'Bloody idiot!'
'Get a doctor!'
'He just kept right on - didn't even stop!'
Why doesn't the ambulance come and stop this screaming?

Which one is screaming? The one lying on the crossing,
With her head smashed to pieces - or her sister - forced to watch?

Drawing the curtains against the noise,
The September sun reflecting off the cars below.
People crowding round - so called civilised people -
Their blood lust revealed.
Little children watching the stains on the road grow larger.
Their parents judging the tragedy by the amount of mess on the road.
Not taking into account the mother waiting at home -
Completely unaware of the shock she has to bear.
Weeks of despair, self-hatred, and sleeping tablets if she dies.
Years of the same if she lives after this.

The ambulance comes and the screaming stops.
But the agony is only just beginning for me.
The people outside cover their delight at the excitement with
Meaningless platitudes and 'if onlys'.
The cars start to move, the police begin to measure the road,
And the unsightly debris of the accident is concealed.

Saturday returns to normal, but not for me.
'No thank you I don't want any dinner now -
Maybe I'll eat it later'.

Sheila Matthews

What Work To Go To

Six 'til two . . . two 'til ten . . . ten 'til six.
An endless cycle of shifts in the black pit,
A cycle of endless shifts.
In winter, sometimes scarcely glimpsing light
In the short minutes from two 'til dark.
Almost a two mile walk to get to work,
Then walking, bending, crawling underground
Almost the two miles back.

On winter nights I sometimes woke
As the metal catch on the metal gate
Clanged shut, and he was gone
Through the dark, to the dark,
Leaving me lying, wondering
If he'd come back. At certain times
He manned the pit alone, checking the pumps
In velvet dark,
Six 'til two 'til ten 'til six.

Geoff Hunter

THE GIFT OF LIFE

At the beginning I was given the *gift of life*
From then to the end would measure my worth
What I said, what I thought, what I left behind would decide
If I were to be given the answer, to that *gift of life*,

The early days were dedicated by my parents and their ways
Then, with dependence, self reliance, responsibility
                                                          came the question
How to live my life that I would be able to find the answer
The certain way was to know how I had used this *gift of life*

To speak truth, give loyalty devotion and love
For my life must be lived as payment of this gift from above
I do not go to church, but I am no heathen for I have faith
This I hope will lead me to the answer I seek
By my actions and deeds and my thoughts overall

Where do I look, the Bible, the Church, or in my heart
From the Holy man, Pastor, Rabbi or Priest, or the life
                                                          I lead on the way,
How I act, think or the way that I pray
Will I hope lead me to the true story of life,

When the answer comes, will it also signal the end,
Have I passed the test of this *gift of life*
Will it be at the last gasp of breath
Will that be the judgement, the true aim of life,

The one fact of life that I have so far found true
Is the love of my family and that of my wife
Without them I'm nothing, been nothing, left nothing,
This one certain truth is to me part of the answer
Their love alone has taught me the true *gift of life*.

Anibas

MISSING PERSON - PERSON FOUND

Are you there? Did I hear you call?
No, you've gone from here, so far away.
But I turn at the sound of your footstep behind me -
There's no-one there.

I see your place at the table -
Empty now,
Your favourite chair -
Undisturbed.

I talk of 'we' and 'us'
As if it were still yesterday,
And include you in all the family occasions -
Still counting.

But you've gone from here, so far away,
And I must be me, not part of us.
Though I know we will meet again one day,
What shall I do now? There's a void to fill,
A journey to take on an unknown road,
Which, reluctantly, I must begin.

No retreat to the past, to the safe, known way,
But forward with courage and faith,
Where Jesus holds out His hand to me,
Saying, 'I will not let you go.'

Joy Jenkins

THE TRENCHES - LEST WE FORGET

We remember you, you who marched away,
Young brave and proud,
Marching and singing, husbands and sons,
We've took the 'King's shilling' you said.
It seemed the right thing to do at the start,
Kitted out in khaki, all smart, clean and new,
Kit bags, gas masks and guns.
We are ready to give 'em what for you said,
No white feathers for you.
Red, white and blue the Union Jacks fly, giving
                              the spirits a lift.
Woodbines and Lucifers stuffed into pockets
God knows you will need them, all in good time.
Trenches waiting and ready, free board and
                              lodging for all.
When your turn comes you'll go over the top,
Hell can be no worse than this.
Gun fire, barbed wire, you run straight ahead,
Comrades fall by your side.
If you were lucky, your chance came again,
We'll try to do better next time! Next time! Next time!
The Last Post is sounded again, as comrades
                              are laid to rest.
In foreign fields, alien and bare
We will remember you, we who care.
At the foot of memorials everywhere
With poppies as red as the blood you shed,
On that day long ago.

Margaret Lumsden

Does Springtime Still Come To The City?

Some day, will a child ask at his Grandad's knee,
'Please what is springtime, will you tell me?'
'Springtime, darling child, is when bright flowers bloom
And birds sing in the trees. And birds sing in the trees.'

The boy tried hard to understand,
'How can that be, I mean in this land,
Where the cars come and go all the time?
Will the joy of springtime come here where we live?'

Granddad looked out at the things men had made,
Seeing all grimy, forlorn, and decayed;
'Spring, I recall, is when all is made new -
So it was when I was a boy. So it was when I was a boy.'

On through the years, who will explain
How man built and destroyed much for gain?
Things not showing profit, they sought to change;
One day, things they built may just crumble away?

The springtime renewal of hope and of life
Is not in man-made things.
Continuously care for all that we have,
With space where spring can be seen, as Nature ordains.

Doris Payne

FROM ABOVE THE SKY

The radio switched on and it was announced
that in the next couple of weeks we would be
passing through a meteor field and should we
like to see a spectacular sight we would need
to endeavour to look skyward at night.

But as the evening light faded I struggled to stay
awake, sleep slowly taking full effect then awaking
before dawn and looking out of glazed windows -
those were my eyes - no sign of the falling 'stars'.

However my family seven miles away living
close to the ocean breeze saw several thro sleepy
eyes but they had spied those elusive meteors falling;
apparently some just fell - no sign of a tail but
three gave a sight to see, with a sparkling tail and
a bright shimmering head both clearly seen in the
darkness of the night.

We are now the eleventh night and returning home
I once again gazed skyward and onward as far as I
could see and yes there was one no two and three,
my determination had paid off, a sight to see.

The twelfth night is promised to be the best of the
show, so early back home we must go and eyes
upward and head craned to see - but I suggest you
lay flat on the back and feel relaxed and free -
free as the falling stars that might come flying
towards you and a very stiff-necked me.

A space wonder!

Anita Bowditch

UNABLE TO LABEL DISABLED

Discharged into the harmonious chaos of a Tesco car park,
Where the orange badge fails,
Completely,
To impress before the assembled crowd.
A temporary inconvenience fighting to establish
A sudden and distinct capacity
For incapacity.
Proving,
A suitable case for treatment,
And benefit a being,
Unable to label disabled.

John Brook

WHAT AM I

Born to live
only to die
a contradiction
or a lie.
Endeavouring to understand,
failing to see,
the point, the
I, the real me.

My body cells die
and are renewed all through life
so where is the I,
the real me.
It is not this body
that I can see,
the brain is the part
of my anatomy
where I store my memory
yet it is not the I
that is me.

Therefore, when my body
is gone the I that is me
will carry on.
No matter what shape
or form I may be,
the I am,
will always be.

Pauline Dring

ANCHOR BOOKS
SUBMISSIONS INVITED
SOMETHING FOR EVERYONE

ANCHOR BOOKS GEN - Any subject, light-hearted clean fun, nothing unprintable please.

THE OPPOSITE SEX - Have your say on the opposite gender. Do they drive you mad or can we co-exist in harmony?

THE NATURAL WORLD - Are we destroying the world around us? What should we do to preserve the beauty and the future of our planet - you decide!

All poems no longer than 30 lines.
Always welcome! No fee!
Plus cash prizes to be won!

Mark your envelope (eg *The Natural World*)
And send to:
Anchor Books
Remus House, Coltsfoot Drive
Peterborough, PE2 9JX

OVER £10,000 IN POETRY PRIZES TO BE WON!

Send an SAE for details on our New Year 2001 competition!